MOURNE MEN and the U-BOATS 1914 -1918

Matt Maginnis

M.R Maginnis

First published 2013
Reprinted 2017, with corrections and additional material
by M&H Maginnis
Email: mattmaginnis@btinternet.com

ISBN 978-0-9926664-1-5

Printed in Northern Ireland by
Edenderry Print Management
Unit 10b, Argyle Business Centre
39 North Howard Street
Belfast, BT13 2AU

Tel: +44 (0)28 90740192
Email: edenderrydesign2@btconnect.com

FRONT COVER	Submarine Painting by Matt Maginnis
BACK COVER	Author with U19 Deck Gun, Bangor, Co Down

PREFACE

MOURNE MEN and THE U-BOATS 1914 – 1918

The genesis of this work was a chance telephone conversation with my cousin, Wilma Crozier, in the autumn of 2010. She told me a tale about Captain James Ferguson and his encounter with a German U-Boat in 1917. James Ferguson was her husband Alan's grandfather and Alan subsequently expanded on the story. I started to investigate the details further in Kilkeel, Belfast and London and the additional stories I heard about U-Boats from relatives, old friends and new friends led to the production of this book about Mourne merchant seamen and fishermen. The book is written mainly for the family and maritime historian and I hope that it will encourage people in Mourne to delve deeper into their family history and record family events and photographs carefully for future generations.

I have included the story of a famous Mourne Doctor in this 2nd Edition because it gives a different perspective to the U-Boat war and the shadows cast on family life by World War I.

Many people in Mourne, Belfast, Dublin, Dundalk and London helped me with my research. I have tried to mention them all individually at the end of each chapter and I trust that I have not overlooked anybody, because the book could not have been written without their help and expertise. Finally, the book has been a family effort and I am especially grateful for the advice, encouragement and graphical skills given by my wife, Hilary, over the six years of research and writing.

I hope these pages present a sympathetic portrayal of the ghosts they evoke.

I dedicate this book to the family – past, present and future.

M. R. Maginnis

October 2017

CONTENTS

INTRODUCTION

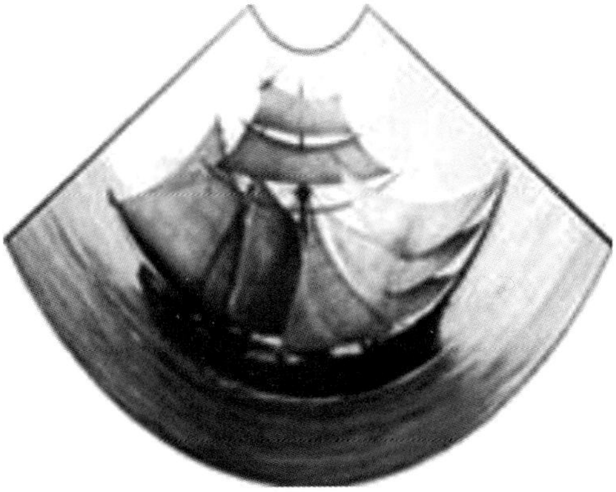

MOURNE SCHOONERMEN & THE STORM

In 1911, the Mourne schooner men had to do battle with the force of the elements. Sometimes they won and sometimes they lost.

At the beginning of November 1911, the British Isles were being pummelled by a series of winter storms accompanied by stinging rain. Telegraph poles were flattened and slates and chimney pots fell on shoppers in Royal Avenue, Belfast. Windows were blown in, awnings were twisted and hoardings rattled before breaking loose. Cross channel steamers were delayed or postponed. Twenty-four sailing vessels had sought shelter in Belfast Lough, in the hope that they could ride out the storm in a few days. Two of the schooners were from Mourne, ELLEN MYVANWY owned by Robert Hamilton of Annalong and TRIAL owned by Mr S. McVeigh of Kilkeel.

The big storm of 5th November 1911 had different outcomes for these two vessels. The ELLEN MYVANWY had three hands on board ~ John Hill as Master, Alexander Gordon as Mate and William Marks as Seaman. The schooner had been on a voyage to Whitehaven but had to seek refuge in Belfast Lough on the 27th October 1911 because of the inclement weather. The Master picked a safe anchorage off Whitehouse Roads. By Sunday 5th November at 10.30 am there was a full tide, a wind approaching hurricane force from the WSW (west-southwest) and storm waves pounding the schooner. The ship was riding with 50 fathoms of chain out on the starboard anchor and 65 fathoms out on the port anchor, when both chains snapped. The Master and crew hoisted a foresail with three reefs to help sail the vessel ashore. The powerful wind almost overturned the schooner a couple of times and onlookers on the shore thought she was going to turn turtle. Miraculously she righted herself and the crew fought to keep her head into the wind but bit-by-bit the vessel was driven towards the shore on the other side of the lough.

At 11.00 am large crowds had gathered at Holywood to see this spectacle of wind and waves versus the schooner men. By 11.30 am, the schooner lost the battle and struck the coast at Seapark, Marino near Holywood. At first, she was driven up the sea wall and one of the crew lowered himself by chain into the water. He managed to scramble ashore.

The two other men on board waited till the vessel swung round and the bowsprit came right across the footpath and they were able to jump ashore. Shortly after the gale increased in strength and the high seas lifted the schooner high and dry onto the footpath.

She was badly damaged as she had hit a channel buoy on the way in to the Holywood side. This schooner had snapped cables, one 2 inches thick and the other 1¾ inches. Her 7 cwt (hundredweight) anchors could not hold her. This Mourne vessel became a total wreck and provided a new tourist attraction at Seapark, Holywood.

The TRIAL was subjected to the same incessant battering by wind and wave as the ELLEN MYVANWY. This schooner was registered at 91 tons and was sailing light with about 6 tons of ballast. The Master was Thomas Lowe who was assisted by James Lowe as Mate and William Curlett as Seaman. They had planned to sail for Workington, but like the other schooners, had sought shelter in Belfast Lough between Garmoyle and Whitehouse. She had been lying there with two anchors out for about ten days very close to the ELLEN MYVANWY. Her problems with the storm started much earlier at 1.30 am when the wind was WSW to West by North. There were 60 fathoms of chain out on the starboard anchor and 45 fathoms of chain on the port anchor. As the wind increased, the Master let out more chain, about 7½ fathoms on each anchor, and he threw out a stream anchor with 60 fathoms of rope attached. By 3 am the vessel began to drive and the Master had no option but to let out more chain. The storm wind increased and, at 10.30 am, the starboard chain parted followed an hour later by the port chain. The Master adopted the same plan of action as the ELLEN MYVANWY. He hoisted a double-reefed foresail and the standing jib with the same objective to beach the ship. The spectators at Holywood were treated to a second show of a Mourne schooner in peril. At first, she seemed destined for the rocks at Rockport, but by skilful seamanship she ended up safely beached at Mitchel's Bay. A couple of anchors were attached to hold her in place and when the tide went out the three members of the crew waded ashore, where members of the Royal North of Ireland Yacht Club rendered assistance to the half-drowned crew.

By 9.30 am on 7th November 1911, the TRIAL was re-floated at Mitchel's Bay, Craigavad by Captain Cooper's tug, HARBOUR LIGHT, with Captain Dempsey performing the delicate operation. The TRIAL was successfully towed to Queen's Quay for inspection and found to be sound with no serious damage. This was a lucky escape for the schooner and she lived to sail another day.

Captain James Doyles's schooner, WHL (WHITE HAIRED LASS), was in trouble during the same storm at Rostrevor. He had been discharging coal at Rostrevor Quay when two chains and several manila ropes snapped. The schooner was beaten about by the storm and carried against the wall in front of the Great Northern Railway Company's Hotel. The backwash saved her from being smashed to pieces and she had to be re-floated later when the storm abated. These sample stories give the reader some idea of the perils facing the schooner crews and show quite clearly why some voyages, although appearing purely routine in a logbook, could last far longer because of the onslaught of the wind heading for Beaufort Force 12.

On the continent, a political storm was deepening and the isobars of empire were set to shift as new alliances were created and others destroyed. London was the capital of the largest empire the world had ever seen, in large part due to the Merchant Seamen trading to all parts of the globe. Rivals were emerging, namely Berlin, Vienna and St. Petersburg. Nobody paid much political attention to the Balkans. In 1880, Lloyd's had recorded over 11,500 sailing vessels and only 2,000 steamers. This imbalance between sail and steam was quickly changing at the start of the First World War. The schooners and ketches of Mourne were competing more frequently now with the increasing number of steamers from Newry, Dundrum and Dundalk. This was a transitional time for the age of sail. After the war by 1930, the balance had totally shifted and Lloyds recorded 210 sailing vessels and 12,000 steamers. Some of the fishing boats in Kilkeel, Ardglass and Portavogie harbours had also realised the power of the engine and abandoned the use of the wind in the interests of greater efficiency and production.

THE STEAMSHIPS

Merchant seamen and their steam coasters have been largely sidelined in the annals of naval history. Their role in carrying essential cargo to other ships and cities has been neglected and undervalued. The civilian and military population all required coal, food supplies, ore, slates, cotton, stone and other basic raw materials. During the First World War, life went on thanks to the trade by merchant seamen. The steam coasters or 'tramps' used, varied in size and draught and the owners tried to have a variety of tonnage and length related to port destinations and estuaries.

On the Irish Sea routes during the 1914 - 1918 War there were numerous operators such as John Kelly and his collier fleet. His fleet was the subject of many famous paintings by Joseph William Carey, which still adorn many sitting room walls in Northern Ireland. The Kelly shipping empire expanded to acquisitions of R. McCowen & Sons Ltd. of Tralee and Alexander King Ltd. of Belfast. DERRYMORE, KERRYMORE and CORBET were well known ship names. John Milligan however, remained independent and his ships were easily remembered because they always ended in 'een', like 'KATHLEEN' and 'BRIDEEN'. Hugh Craig was another Belfast coal importer who diversified by carrying fruit and vegetables from the Channel Islands to Liverpool in the summer months.

Other companies with their specialised cargoes and history were the Antrim Iron Ore Company Limited of Belfast operating from Red Bay; the Neill family of Bangor used steamers to bring coal to Bangor; the East Downshire Steam Ship Company Limited sailed from Dundrum and had to negotiate a tricky harbour entrance; Joseph Fisher of Newry another busy ship-owner with his trademark tree names for his ships such as YEWS and MANGO; Samuel Lockington & Co. sailed from Dundalk and competed with the bigger steamers like the SS DUNDALK; Robert Tidcastle operated from Dublin along with Arthur

Guinness, the Dublin brewers who used steamers to carry casks of stout to England. The Dundalk and Newry Steam Packet Company carried passengers and cattle to Scotland and England. Howdens of Larne were also in the coal business and operated four ships at the onset of the war in 1914. There were also steam coaster companies in Bray, Wexford, Limerick, Sligo and Londonderry.

COLLISIONS

Sometimes the competition and conflict between sail and steam power manifested itself in painful and tragic collisions. LADY LILFORD (1911) and MISS HUGHES (1917) from Kilkeel were both involved in serious collisions with steamers. LADY LILFORD will be mentioned in a later chapter on Captain James Ferguson, but the ketch MISS HUGHES will be covered here.

MISS HUGHES was a sailing ketch owned by Robert Green of Kilkeel and John Chambers was the Master. It had been built at Carnarvon in 1884 and was registered at 65 gross tons. On Monday 8th January 1917, it had been on a voyage from Girvan to Belfast with a cargo of coal on board. After sheltering at Campbeltown for a few days, the ketch was propelled swiftly south by a NNE (north-northeast) wind to Kilroot Point by 3.30 pm. She was all set for the Pilot Boat with all lights burning and headed up the channel. When the ketch was near No. 7 Buoy, the steamer WHEATSHEAF was spotted bearing down on MISS HUGHES from No. 10 Buoy. The Pilot ordered the helm to be put hard a port but the steamer hit the ketch amidships with her port bow. The sailing vessel began to sink in a few minutes and the three-man crew, all from Annalong: John Chambers, Master (32 yrs old); John McVeigh, Mate (55 yrs old) and James Heaney, Able Seaman (23 yrs old) plus the Pilot scrambled for the lifeboat. This was pointless as the lifeboat had got caught in the rigging and quickly filled with water. The four men clung to the rigging and were rescued by a lifeboat from the steamer. Thankfully they were all landed safely in Belfast.

Such collisions were commonplace during this transitional period before the dominance of steam power. The Masters ensured that there were regular lifeboat drills and inspection of lights and lifesaving equipment.

1914 THE ONSET OF WAR

It is hard to believe that a wrong turn by a chauffeur on the 28th June 1914 in Sarajevo would precipitate the start of the First World War and the death and displacement of millions of people on a global scale. The Archduke Franz Ferdinand, a symbol of the Austro-Hungarian Empire, was a hated figure by the Black Hand gang, a Serb nationalist terrorist cell. They tried to bomb him at first but failed. Later one of the conspirators, Gavril Princip, came across the Archduke's car, which had fatefully taken a wrong turn. He opened fire with his Browning 9 mm semi-automatic pistol and shot the Archduke and his pregnant wife Sophie at close range.

The seismic shock waves from this assassination gradually spread from the epicentre in the Balkans and tipped Europe into war. By August 1914, Germany was at war on two fronts, Russia to the East and Belgium/France to the West. Britain declared war on the 4th August 1914 and this was to be fought on the land, in the air and on the sea. The Mourne area, like all parts of the British Isles, was the setting for recruiting drives and young men enlisted to do their bit for King and Country. In the harbours of Mourne, the schooners and ketches of Annalong and Kilkeel plied their trade in granite sets and potatoes across the Irish Sea in exchange for coal from the coalfields of Central Scotland, South Wales and Lancashire. They could reach the smaller harbours and jetties along the County Down coast, which have long disappeared. Places like Millbay, Derryogue Harbour, Glassdrumman and Greencastle.

Elsewhere the British Navy mustered its dreadnoughts and battlecruisers and at the outset they outnumbered the German opposition. It was the same where submarines were concerned. In 1914, Britain had 73 submarines compared with Germany's 33 Unter See Boots. However, only 18 of the British submarines had overseas capability whereas the Germans had 28. Initially the U-Boats were powered by paraffin burners or heavy-duty oil, but after 1913, with the launch of the U19 followed by the infamous U21, the diesel engine proved to be the most successful. This engine produced less smoke when running on the surface and gave the U-Boat a greater range beyond the North Sea into the Irish Sea and Atlantic shipping lanes. The U-Boats had a superior periscope designed by Zeiss and a powerful new explosive in their torpedoes. Telefunken wireless transmitters with a range of over 140 miles gave them another advantage over the British. By 1915, Germany started to mass-produce the smaller UB class of U-Boat for use in coastal waters and the UC class for sowing mines in the approaches to British ports.

Both sides adopted blockade tactics using this new technology and brought the submarine into contact with the merchantmen and fishermen of Mourne. This contact sometimes ended in courteous exchanges, contested mystery, black humour and sadly human tragedy. The Mourne Men risked their lives at sea against the elements and the underwater predators armed with their deadly silverfish. This book hopefully tells the story of some of them and their courage during their close encounters with the U-Boats.

Kilkeel Harbour 2012

SOURCES OF INFORMATION

1 Public Record Office Northern Ireland; CUS1/5/1/2
Wreck Depositions 1908 - 1922

2 Belfast Evening Telegraph; 6th November 1911
(Photo of the ELLEN MYVANWY Wreck Page 5)

3 Belfast Evening Telegraph; 7th November 1911

4 Northern Whig; 6th November 1911 Page 7 and 8

5 Belfast News Letter; 6th November 1911 Page 7

6 National Archives, Kew BT99/3287 (MISS HUGHES)

Annalong Harbour 2012

The Mourne Mountains from Carlingford Lough

"SORRY
BUT WAR IS WAR!"

THE SINKING OF THE KILCOAN 30th JANUARY 1915

This story came to light because my grandfather Robert Charles Maginnis and his brother John 'Storm' Maginnis were crewmembers of the KILCOAN steamer from Larne. The Maginnis family in Kilkeel had many versions of this incident and this article is my attempt to establish the facts and find out what happened on that day in 1915.

On the morning of Saturday 30th January 1915, the brothers were working on board the KILCOAN, a Howden steamer from Larne. The Master, James Meneely, was waiting patiently for the fog on the Mersey to lift. On the same day in Belfast, you could visit the Grand Opera House and watch the last performance of the pantomime, 'Dick Whittington' or go to the cinema to laugh at Charlie Chaplin or the Keystone Cops. The Shelbourne football team was getting ready to play Glentoran at the Oval and Campbell College was about to do battle with Foyle College in school rugby at Ormeau. At sea, merchant ships were loaded with essential cargoes and arrivals from Glasgow, Ardrossan, Heysham, Cardiff and Garston brought in cargoes of rye, flour, coal, steel plate and tiles. English coal was being sold for 32 shillings a ton and Scottish coal for 28 shillings a ton. There was a discount for cash! Further afield, Andrew Mulholland from Kilkeel who was the brother-in-law of Robert Charles Maginnis, was south of Ypres with the Royal Irish Fusiliers. Like a lot of young Mourne men, he had joined up at the outbreak of war and, by the end of January 1915, he was fighting the Germans from trenches east of Vierstraat dodging sniper fire and shrapnel, strengthening defences with sandbags and barbed wire, and protecting himself from frostbite. The Irish Sea ports seemed a long way from the battle fronts at Ypres and Soissons. However, that degree of complacency was soon to change with the arrival of a U-Boat in the Irish Sea.

U21

Otto Hersing, commander of the U21 was selected by the German navy to extend the zone of submarine warfare into the Irish Sea and possibly attempt to blockade a major port – Liverpool. He left Wilhelmshaven on the 21st January 1915 and picked his way through the defensive screen at the Dover Straits and the mine-strewn English Channel, round Land's End to the Welsh Coast. He was sighted by an armed drifter in Cardigan Bay but proceeded north to Holyhead and then Walney Island. This was an eight-mile-long island with an airship shed, shipbuilding works and munitions factories. Vickers had established airship production there and in Barrow-in-Furness since 1908.

KILCOAN (Painting courtesy of Norman Whitla)

Hersing had a cool nerve and a good reputation as a U-Boat commander and his main claim to fame was his sinking of the H.M.S. PATHFINDER off Abbs Head in the North Sea on the 5th September 1914. His actions on the 29th January 1915 are more debatable and perhaps foolhardy. At 1.50 pm the conning tower of a large submarine was spotted in the bay heading for shallow water and in the lookout post there was some confusion about its identity. At 2.25 pm the submarine made its presence clear by firing a shell at the New Airship shed. The U21 had announced its arrival in the Irish Sea theatre of war totally ignorant of the fact that she was staring down the barrels of a battery of six-inch guns! Was this an act of madness on Hersing's part or was he just testing coastal defences?

The submarine was within range of the battery and after a second shot from the intruder the battery returned fire. Manned by No. 7 Company of the Lancashire and Cheshire Royal Garrison Artillery they aimed eleven rounds at the U-Boat. The firing continued for five minutes causing vibrations and consternation in local houses. The impudent intruder realising he was in range of the guns as the first shells screamed over the sub, decided to crash dive and head for deeper water. The battery commander said the submarine was not an easy target because of the smoke. The rate of fire was slow but some witnesses claimed a hit. This unfortunately turned out to be inaccurate.

The battery was criticised by the Admiralty on paper for its inaction since it failed to identify the sub in the first half hour. "It watched the vessel for half an hour and did nothing." There was "no excuse for delay" in taking action. This encounter marks the start of the U-Boat war in the Irish Sea and the U21 had chalked up another first. It was the first U-Boat to sink a warship by torpedo and now it was the first U-Boat to enter the Irish Sea and it was about to create havoc and panic between Liverpool and Belfast. The U21 was just like a fox let loose in a crowded poultry yard.

SS BEN CRUACHAN

The BEN CRUACHAN was a steel hulled steamer of 1,978 tons owned by the Morrison Shipping Company of Newcastle-on-Tyne. The ship was rigged fore and aft and had been built at Stockton in 1902. The crew on Saturday 30th January 1915 numbered 23 including the Master David W. Heggie.

She was carrying a cargo of coal for the British Admiralty and had left Scapa Flow on the 28th January intending to reach Liverpool by the afternoon of the 30th January. The wind was a light southwest one and the sea fairly calm. She did not spot the U21 creeping up on her until it was too late.

This steamer had left Cardiff on the 14th December 1914 for Scapa Flow under contract to the Admiralty for coaling ships there. There was 4000 tons of coal on board and the Captain was ordered to take 1000 tons back to Liverpool. Alex Laing, 47 years old from Aberdeen was usually the Master. However, he took sick and left the ship at sea on the 19th January 1915 off the North of Scotland where he was transferred to a hospital ship. David Heggie, the Mate, took over command on the same date. He had sealed orders from the Admiralty on board.

Fifteen miles NW of the NW Lightship in Liverpool Bay the steamer was overtaken and stopped by the U21 at 10.30 am. They were given ten minutes to abandon ship and they were advised to get all their belongings off the steamer, especially their money. There was an immediate scamper to fill kitbags and launch two small boats. When the lifeboats were alongside the submarine, the Master was forced to go back on board the steamer with an armed guard to collect the ship's papers. The Germans attached a kind of mine to the BEN CRUACHAN and collected the charts and papers for scrutiny. The fuse was lit and the mine exploded causing the ship to start sinking almost immediately. Otto Hersing, apologetic in tone, expressed regret that he had to blow up the vessel but "War is war". He questioned Master D. Heggie who was normally the Mate on this vessel. The acting captain was asked where they were headed and where they had discharged coal. He hoped that the crew would be picked up before bad weather set in, shook hands with the captain and saluted. The Mate of the BEN CRUACHAN remarked:

"The German officers were very gentlemanly. I give them credit for that."

The ship was sinking stern first and the crew, cold but safe in the small boats, were directed to sail towards a trawler and they were picked up by the fishing boat MARGARET an hour or so later and taken to Fleetwood by 6.00 pm.
The sinking of the BEN CRUACHAN caused a sensation in Fleetwood and a number of steam fishing trawlers fishing ten miles north of the Lune Buoy made a hasty return to port. After 6.00 pm, word spread that the U-Boats had arrived in the Irish Sea and the rumours of possible attacks had become a reality.

The crewmembers of the BEN CRUACHAN were looked after by the Distressed Mariners Society and were quickly given a warm meal. Unfortunately, they would soon receive more customers.
In terms of submarine warfare, the sinking of the BEN CRUACHAN was not only the first major incident in the Irish Sea but a very serious one, which caused alarm in Admiralty circles.

A NEAR MISS

The SS KATHLEEN owned by Messrs Milligan & Company of Belfast had left Manchester at 5.00 pm Friday evening with a cargo of 900 tons of coal for Belfast. The SS LINDA BLANCHE was in her company down the canal. Fog slowed the journey in the Mersey and she anchored at Sloyne (near Cammel Laird's shipyard at Birkenhead) and got underway again at 8.00 am on Saturday morning. She passed the LINDA BLANCHE 20 miles north of the Bar Lightship and she witnessed the BEN CRUACHAN going down by the stern. Edward Doran an AB (Able Seaman) of the KATHLEEN said that the BEN CRUACHAN was on their lee starboard going down by the stern and the bow stood upright out of the water.
Speed and fog obscured the view and Captain J.T. Paysden who lived at Brookvale House, Park Avenue, Strandtown decided to take evasive action as he could see the sub half a mile away. He called for full steam ahead and the

stokers worked overtime as the steamer headed for Douglas in the Isle of Man. The KATHLEEN faded into the haze and disappeared from sight. The submarine now turned its attention to the LINDA BLANCHE, which was following the same course.

The KATHLEEN reported the incident to the pilot at Douglas but failed to signal the SS GRAPHIC because of a sleet shower, which rendered it impossible to warn the passenger ship five miles away. The SS GRAPHIC had left Belfast at 7.30 am and carried 100 passengers and 40 crew on board bound for Liverpool.

She was heading straight into the danger zone. The SS KATHLEEN successfully completed her voyage and berthed in the Abercorn Basin at 8.00 am on Sunday morning, much to the delight of her owners.

SS LINDA BLANCHE

Lord Penrhyn of Bangor, Co. Caernarvon (Anglesey Steamship Company) owned the SS LINDA BLANCHE; she was rigged as a three master and carried a general cargo for the Belfast Steam Ship Company. The cargo was about 300 tons and made up of oil, woollens, hair, paper, drapery, cottons, steel rails and 70 tons of firebricks and iron works for the Belfast Gas Works. The ship had left Manchester on the 29th January and was heading northwest on roughly the same course as the SS KATHLEEN. It was now midday and the sea rated smooth with a slight haze. The U21 stopped her and the eleven merchant men were given 10 minutes to abandon ship. Master John Ellis ordered the lowering of two small boats, which were steered towards the submarine. The crew in their haste to board the lifeboats overlooked the skipper's fox terrier. The little dog had to make a massive jump into the sea and swim to the lifeboats to be reunited with his master. A German boarding party then planted two bombs on board the LINDA BLANCHE, one in the bridge and one in the forecastle. All documents relating to the cargo and ship were taken by the Germans along with two of the charts. The Master and crew were then cast adrift from the submarine and directed to sail towards a fishing vessel in the distance. In an hour, they were picked up and rescued by the steam trawler NIBLICK and taken to Fleetwood.

According to newspaper reports the crew of the LINDA BLANCHE paid tribute to the courtesy of the German officers who said:

"Sorry - but war is war." The crewmembers of the steamer were offered cigars and cigarettes as an act of compensation. The German officers were very considerate and ensured that there was enough water and provisions on board the lifeboats.

SS KILCOAN

The KILCOAN was a Howden steamer from Larne. The company can be traced back to 1830 when John Smiley of Inver, Larne commenced business as a coal and grain merchant with premises at Bank Quays, Larne. This firm was successful and transferred to three nephews of John Smiley, namely John, Matthew and Charles Howden. They carried on the business as Howden Brothers based around the small jetty at the Bank Quays and Larne harbour. They had offices in Dunluce Street, Larne. At the turn of the last century, the brothers all passed away and Howdens was handed over to their nephews, William J. R. Harbinson and Charles L. MacKean. In 1915, they operated a fleet of four ships: ROMA built 1903, MONARCH built 1884, CARNDUFF built 1910 and finally KILCOAN built 1905.

The KILCOAN had been built as a cargo steamer by the Ailsa Shipbuilding Company in Troon. It was registered as 456 tons and powered by a compound expansion engine, which drove a single shaft. Before the war, the KILCOAN was heavily involved in the coasting trade to a variety of destinations from the Larne base to Garston, Bristol, Lydney on the Severn, Ayr, Maryport, Barrow, Glasgow, Troon, Fleetwood, Ellesmere Port, Briton Ferry, Runcorn,

Manchester, Liverpool, Whitehaven, Port Talbot, Dublin, Swansea, Cork, Waterford, Partington on the Manchester Ship Canal and Sligo. A lot were coal ports where loads were picked up for Larne, Belfast and elsewhere.

In 1913 the KILCOAN completed 202 voyages with Captain Meneely as Master, John Boyd as Mate and J.F. Ainley as Chief Engineer. Wages were related to rank and responsibility on the ship with the Chief Engineer receiving £3 5s 0d per week, 2nd Engineer £2 2s 6d per week, Mate £2 2s 6d per week, Lamp Trimmer £1 14s 6d per week and the ABs (Able Seamen) £1 12s 6d per week. This all sounds a paltry sum nowadays, but before the First World War, these figures were above the minimum wage.

On the 30th January 1915, the KILCOAN was on a coal run from Garston on the Mersey to Belfast. Her captain, James Meneely, lived in University Avenue, Belfast and he had a ten-man crew on board to help him run the ship. Captain Meneely was originally from Islandmagee like three others on the ship.

These men were all rated highly in terms of ability and conduct, most had served on the ship since 1914. Two of the crew were members of the Maginnis family from Harbour Road, Kilkeel. The brothers John and Robert Charles Maginnis.

KILCOAN CREW LIST 1915

Names	Age	Nationality	Birthplace
Master James Meneely	52	British	Islandmagee
James Niblock, Mate	N/A	British	Islandmagee
John Maginnis, Seaman	42	British	Kilkeel
Charlie Maginnis, Seaman	28	British	Kilkeel
Andrew Niblock Seaman	50	British	Islandmagee
William McGrady, Boy	15	British	Islandmagee
John McAuley, Cook	25	British	Liverpool

J.F Ainley, Chief Engineer	49	British	Belfast
Saul Montgomery, 2nd Engineer	38	British	Belfast
W.J. Bamford, Fireman	34	British	Belfast
Bernard Fee, Fireman	N/A	British	Belfast

John was nicknamed 'Storm' and was born on the 6th June 1871. His younger brother Robert Charles, known as Charlie, was born on the 21st August 1882 and lived halfway down the Harbour Road for most of his life. Charlie was small in stature and sported a moustache. They were the sons of James Maginnis and Esther Teggarty who were married on 3rd September 1870 in Kilkeel. By 1915, the brothers were experienced seamen who had served their time on many sailing ships and steamers. Before the war, the two brothers worked together on the same sailing ships. John, older and more experienced, was the Master of the EXCEL ketch, owned by Andrew Robinson of Annalong in 1911. This small vessel had been registered in Poole, Dorset with a 77-gross tonnage. John was assisted by Joseph Chambers as Mate from Annalong, Charlie Maginnis as an AB and Richard Moore as Cook. They were well-acquainted with the Irish Sea ports such as Liverpool, Maryport, Dublin, Ayr, Barrow, Troon and Rostrevor.

ROBERT CHARLES MAGINNIS

Before the EXCEL, they sailed on a small Annalong cutter, PIUS THE NINTH, which had been registered at 33gt in Dublin. This was another Andrew Robinson ship which was used in the granite trade.

By early 1912, the brothers switched to steamers owned by Fishers of Newry. This was probably for economic reasons; higher wages and more regular work. John became a Mate on the SS ROSTREVOR which had a crew of 12 and Charlie ended up on the SS WALNUT. They were used to the tough life on the steamers and they were resilient, resourceful and skillful in the loading and unloading of the chosen cargo of the day. Sometimes they lodged in Belfast and saw many a scrap in the dockside pubs and inner-city areas. They slept in bunks; usually two tiered in the forecastle and queued for the toilet. There was no privacy on board and every man had a role to play above or below decks. There were davits to inspect, lifeboat drills, hatch covers to maintain, winches to operate and methane and coal dust to avoid. Days were long and arduous depending on the tide and vagaries of the weather. They were perceived as lower class civilian sailors and undervalued by society at large.

The KILCOAN was well cared for by these men and she was rated A1 with a fresh look to her varnish at the start to 1915. On the morning of 30th January 1915, the KILCOAN was fully loaded with coal and waiting for the tide and clear visibility. Her three masts stood proud in the morning light and her black hull was slightly broken by a red boot topping. Her black funnel with a broad deep-red band began to belch smoke as the firemen fed the boilers. She was ready for the return journey to Belfast.

SS KILCOAN

The KILCOAN left Garston at 9.30 am on the flood tide and was off the Bar Lightship at 11.55 am with a course set NW for the Chickens (off the Isle of Man). Captain Meneely came on deck at 12.15 pm and relieved the Mate, James Niblock for dinner. The Mate returned at 12.45 pm and he was left in charge. At 1.30 pm, the sea was rated as slight with a WSW wind and the ship was steaming 18 miles NW of the Bar Lightship. Hersing's U21 sailed alongside displaying a British White Ensign. The Mate, thinking this was a British submarine, shouted below to the Master and said:

"Come on deck. There is a submarine that wishes to speak to us."

This turned out to be the understatement of the day! Captain Meneely went on deck and saw a large submarine with her hull painted a dull white and her bridge and conning tower a darker colour. Machine guns were trained on the steamer and a number of men, estimated at 10 on the conning tower, watched with field glasses and brandished revolvers. There were two sailors with rifles aimed in the direction of the KILCOAN. The British White Ensign was flying from the conning tower and had probably been pinched from one of the previous victims. This flag was removed later on, according to the Captain's report.

Hersing asked Captain Meneely what cargo he was carrying and when he answered coal, the order was given to abandon ship quickly.

"Get into your boats!" he commanded in good English.

The starboard and port lifeboats were launched at speed and all hands boarded. One lifeboat had 6 on board and the other 5. Some had run below to retrieve their personal effects and clothes. Others abandoned ship in what they were wearing. By now, Hersing had established a routine and shouted:

"Come alongside (the sub)" and "Get on board." All on board Captain Meneely's lifeboat were ordered to stand on the deck of the U-Boat.

There was a deck gun smothered in grease behind the conning tower and a large number of armed ratings covering the KILCOAN crew and watching their every move. The crew climbed onto the deck of the sub giving Hersing more leverage. If a destroyer or patrol boat showed up, the KILCOAN crew would slow things down since they would have to swim for it. The next question was: "Have you got the ship's papers?"

The negative reply from the Captain caused an angry response and Meneely was sent to retrieve them accompanied by an armed escort.

They rowed across to the KILCOAN in a well-rehearsed routine. Four armed sailors covered the captain at all times and primed a large bomb with a two-yard fuse. On board Meneely was ordered to collect the ship's papers while the Germans fixed the bomb amidships. The Captain handed over the Ship's Certificate of Registry, Cargo Book and the Custom Coastwise Transire. They asked for the logbook but Meneely said that he did not know where it was. They then took the Union Jack Flag and the Ship's Ensign. The fuse to the bomb was lit and the boarding party headed back to the U21.

The bomb exploded on the return journey and, according to witnesses on the sub, blasted a hole in the port side below the belting. The German Captain seemed to calm down when he received the ship's papers. However, at some point during their time on the deck of the sub, Charlie Maginnis and others were offered cigars and cigarettes by one of the officers. These were refused, as tensions must have been running high, given the treatment of Captain Meneely. Charlie got into an altercation with a German sailor who probably took exception to the refusal of the gift. Charlie, although of medium height, only 5ft 5", would not run away from a fight. Spit was certainly exchanged and the Germans hastened the crew's departure with a few choice words. Somebody asked Storm Maginnis what the German said and he replied in a rough translation: "Get off the ------- sub!"

They were told to row towards a vessel in the distance.

Then a very strange thing happened. The U21 steamed toward the SS GLADYS of the Liverpool Monks Line, which was on a run from Garston to Douglas with coal. The U21 circled the little steamer at first, a manoeuvre which made the crew very nervous but Hersing concluded that it was a steam trawler. At 2.30 pm, Hersing hailed the GLADYS and ordered the captain to rescue the KILCOAN crew! He was making sure the men in the small boats had safe passage before hypothermia struck in the fading winter light. The GLADYS followed the U21 to the lifeboats, which she took in tow. The U21 commander insisted that the

GLADYS steamed towards Douglas on its intended voyage and not back to Liverpool, which was closer.

Obviously Hersing wanted to wait for more ships approaching Liverpool and the Mersey and he did not want the alarm to be raised. William McGrady, the youngest crew member, summed up his experience when interviewed in Douglas; 'I consider that we were very lucky, in being picked up so soon, as to spend the night in an open boat in the cold would have been awful.'

The U-Boat returned to the KILCOAN and using the 105-mm deck gun fired a gunshot into the hull to speed up the sinking. The KILCOAN started to go down at 3.20 pm. The crew of the KILCOAN were saved by the GLADYS and landed at Douglas in the Isle of Man at 10.30 pm with a tale to tell their grandchildren. Captain George Kelly, Harbour Master and agent for the Shipwrecked Mariners' Society, took charge of the crew and found them lodgings at Mr. Lord's Roseberg House. Mr W.J.R. Harbinson (Howden Bros.) received a telegram from Captain Meneely that night which stated:

'KILCOAN SUNK BY SUBMARINE.
CREW SAFE HERE.'

ESCAPE OF THE SS GRAPHIC

Captain Porter of the SS GRAPHIC sighted the KILCOAN going down about 3.30 pm and he knew he was in grave danger 22 miles NW of the Liverpool Bar Lightship. As the KILCOAN slid into the depths with a muffled explosion and a puff of smoke, Porter's ship came across a mass of wreckage floating on the sea. The sea, which had been fairly choppy suddenly, became smoother owing to the presence of an oil slick on the surface. Hundreds of barrels were bobbing and colliding. Boxes of cheese, sides of bacon, crates and sundry goods floated past as witnesses to the earlier destructive path of the U21. Captain Porter instinctively knew there was a submarine about and ordered lifebelts to be issued to all passengers and lifeboats to be made ready. He spotted the sub and changed course immediately. He put the GRAPHIC head to the wind and waves. An extra batch of stokers was put in the stokehold and he raced away from the submarine, which was still stalking his vessel. The U21 submerged and Porter guessed she was trying to rise again in front of him. He adopted a zigzag course on a new heading for Holyhead away from his intended destination, Liverpool.

SS GRAPHIC escapes!

The U-Boat surfaced again, but because of the superior speed of the GRAPHIC, she was outmanoeuvred by Porter's crew and after 20 minutes she gave up the chase. The sea and wind had helped to swamp the sub and she was beaten by Porter's tactics.

There was a great cheer from the passengers when they saw the sub being left in the wake of the GRAPHIC. There was no hint of panic on board given the fact that they had witnessed the destruction and sinking of the KILCOAN. They recognised that Captain Porter had shown remarkable courage and seamanship. The GRAPHIC arrived in Liverpool only 2 hours behind schedule. The passengers assembled on deck and presented the Captain with a hastily written testimonial as a token of their appreciation. He was given a rousing cheer by all and modestly said that he was only doing his duty. The Belfast Steamship Company had lost their chartered ship, the LINDA BLANCHE, but not the GRAPHIC.

AFTERMATH

Otto Hersing was a popular U-Boat commander in his homeland and he was the equivalent of a major celebrity today. Postcards of his submarine, the U21, were sold as German propaganda. He was back at base by 19th February and in one interview to a German newspaper he made sardonic comments with colleagues about the U-Boats having to win the war for the Kaiser. He made light of his Irish Sea expedition and used it to the maximum for propaganda purposes. When asked about the BEN CRUACHAN incident, he said that his lieutenant asked the Master of the doomed ship: "What cargo are you carrying?"

"General cargo", replied the captain.

The German mistook the description for a military personality, then exclaimed: "What! Has he got General Cargo on board?"

This was followed swiftly by: "You have ten minutes to leave the ship with your crew. Bring your ship's papers here!"

After the crew left the steamer, the Germans discovered that the Master had left the papers on board and he had to go back with a four-man guard to retrieve them. This turned out to be no laughing matter for the Admiralty and caused considerable anxiety for the top ranks. Hersing had set out to do a Drake and this was his Cadiz moment. He had succeeded in singeing the King's beard!

There was concern that the papers seized may be of use to the enemy. Charts had been taken and a list of warships coaled at Scapa Flow noted from the logbook. Admiralty documents such as a book of Block Sketches of British, French and German Submarines, Signalling Instructions and a Notice to Mariners were now in enemy hands. The Master had been covered by a revolver at the time and this helped to explain why they had been handed over. Charts had also been taken from the LINDA BLANCHE in a similar operation and this compounded the problem.

The loss of confidential documents placed the merchant seamen in greater danger, especially as the submarine war was heading for a different phase. In 1915, the German U-Boat Commanders showed many acts of humanitarianism and no more than 21% of sinkings were performed without warning.

On Monday 1st February 1915, cross channel steamships were put on hold and left to make their own decisions because of the U21 attacks. Voyages across the Irish Sea were deemed too perilous and sailings remained suspended on 2nd February. Mail from Glasgow was transferred to the shorter Stranraer – Larne route but the mail service using the steamers ULSTER and LEINSTER continued their service. Portholes were darkened and only one headlight shone on these faster boats. The U21 attacks naturally affected insurance rates and premiums soared steeply.

By Wednesday morning 3rd February, the SS GRAPHIC had returned to Belfast after a normal trip from the Mersey. The same company's steamship COMIC reached the port by midday. The Heysham route resumed sailings with the ANTRIM and DONEGAL. Ardrossan and Glasgow boats also arrived. The colliers went back to work despite gale force winds. Sailings returned to normal, however in the depths, the U-Boats were waiting.

The KILCOAN crew had been paid on Monday 1st February and by Wednesday they had managed to get back to Liverpool. Eight of them were on the docks waiting for a trip back to Belfast. The 'Dick Whittington' pantomime company left Belfast on the DONEGAL for Heysham. The mail boats at Holyhead and Kingstown started to deliver again.

The owners of the SS KATHLEEN, overjoyed that their ship had escaped the guns of the U-Boat, presented souvenirs to Captain Paysden, Chief Engineer Cleary and all crewmembers such as David Hutchinson and Edward Doran.

They praised the seamanship and loyalty of the crew, especially the engine room staff and the stokers.

In Germany, the Navy was planning an effective blockade of Britain using U-Boats. By 4th February 1915, the Admirals had won over the Kaiser and the Chancellor and finally they made an announcement:

The waters around Great Britain and Ireland, including the whole of the English Channel, are herewith declared to be in the War Zone. From February 18th onwards, every merchant ship met with in this War zone will be destroyed, nor will it always be possible to obviate the danger with which passengers and crew are thereby threatened.

Neutral ships, too, will run a risk in the War Zone, for in view of the misuse of neutral flags by the British Government on January 31st and owing to the hazards of, it may not always be possible to prevent the attacks meant for hostile ships from being directed against neutral ships.

The reference to January 31st referred to the British Admiralty informing ship owners that the flying of a neutral flag was a recognised ruse de guerre often adopted in the past and not in breach of International Law, providing no hostile act was carried out under cover of the flag. Hersing had already used a ruse de guerre to sneak up on the KILCOAN but he had shown humanity and gave the Merchant Seamen safe passage.

In response on the 10th February 1915, the Admiralty produced a document entitled:

'*Instructions for Owners and Masters of British Merchant Ships issued with reference to the Operations of German Submarines against British Shipping.*'

These instructions included advice on how to minimize the danger from torpedoes; how to be ready for full speed ahead and to plug holes from deck gun damage; how to use false colours and disguises to evade capture; finally, how to find armed assistance at certain listed ports, e.g. Larne and Belfast.

Howdens continued to operate their fleet from Larne Harbour and the Bank Quays. They ordered more steamers such as the SALLAGH, CARGAN, STRAIDE, DROMAINE, FALAVEE, GALGORM and GRACEHILL. Unfortunately, a U-Boat sank the SALLAGH in 1917 off Bardsey Island with the loss of one crewmember. In 1917, Howdens were the honorary agents for the Shipwrecked Mariners Society, a charitable institution tasked with helping seamen in distress. This was a voluntary duty on their part and they guaranteed that every penny donated to the Society would be used for actual relief in relation to food, clothes, lodging, medical treatment and travel home. Howdens saw it as their duty to write to the Secretary at the Admiralty in London on the 5th February 1915. They wanted to inform the Admiralty about certain facts relating to the U21 that had been reported to them by Captain Meneely and his crew.

"The length was about 215 feet; her deck was quite flat, this with her upper works was painted very dark grey, her under part was a dirty white; she steamed on the surface 17 to 18 knots; she had a permanently fixed 8 pounder (3 inch) gun behind the conning tower, the gun was plastered in grease. She carried a crew of 25 men some of which told our men that she had 8 torpedo tubes 2 at the bow, 2 at stern and 2 at each side but our crew say it was impossible to see whether the Germans were speaking the truth as regards this or not."

After this bit of intelligence destined for a sympathetic ear, Howdens got to the punch line. "May we ask what is the proper method for us to adopt to make claim for compensation for our loss as we were not insured against war risk?" This elicited a negative response from the Admiralty with words to the effect: 'That in regard to compensation it is necessary to point out that ship owners who fail to insure their boats have no-one but themselves to blame if a loss is occasioned thereby.'

Howdens had a right to feel aggrieved by this response as a similar request from the owners of the LINDA BLANCHE (Lord Penrhyn) had a more positive outcome. The LINDA BLANCHE was not insured under the Government's War

Risks Insurance Scheme; her claim was noted by the Admiralty for action after the war with a view to obtaining compensation from the German Government. A bit premature since the outcome was not a foregone conclusion in 1915.

Their intelligence report on the U21 was quite accurate. The sub was about 210 feet long with a speed of 15 knots on the surface. She had a 105-mm deck gun, the crew usually numbered 35 men and she carried 6 torpedoes with 2 bow and 2 stern tubes. The U21 was a Type U19 diesel-powered torpedo attack class and there were four boats of this type built at Danzig. It had been launched on the 8th February 1913 and was commanded by Otto Hersing for most of the First World War.

There was an unfortunate sting in the tail for the Howdens in Larne. Alexander King Ltd brought an action against them for damages for breach of charter party made between the plaintiffs and the defendants on the 19th May 1914, for the carriage of coal from Garston to Belfast. This was a 12-month agreement (1st June 1914 until 31st May 1915) for the carrying of 25,000 tons of coal. Howdens had carried out the terms of the agreement until the 30th January 1915 when the KILCOAN was sunk. Howdens intimated their intention, not to carry on with the terms of the agreement since the chosen vessel, the KILCOAN, had been sunk and no other vessel had been chartered by Alexander King to continue delivery of the remainder of the coal. Judgement was entered for the plaintiffs at £920! War is war, but Business is business.

Hersing became a very successful U-Boat commander and was known to colleagues as a 'Destroyer of Battleships'. He had sunk the H.M.S. PATHFINDER and invaded the Irish Sea. He then moved to the Mediterranean war theatre around Gallipoli and sank more warships, four in total. He continued to sink merchant ships as well and he earned the Iron Cross and the Blue Max for his war effort. The U21 survived the war but sank under mysterious circumstances on the way to surrender in Harwich, possibly because the commander ordered the opening of the sub's valves. Otto Hersing survived both World Wars and lived until he was 75 years old. He died on the 5th July 1960 at Oldenburg, Germany.

John and Charlie Maginnis did not take 'time out' after their ordeal. John joined the schooner, LORNE, in Warrenpoint as an AB, just over a week later. He went back across the Irish Sea to Preston where he disembarked and then travelled to Liverpool. Here he joined the rescue vessel, the SS GLADYS, on the 26th February 1915 and worked on board until May. Maybe this was his vote of thanks to the crew that rescued him, after the U21 attack. He returned to Kilkeel and served for a time on the WIZARD at the harbour and later the WILLIAM & MARY, owned by Edward Tyrrell from Arklow.

Charlie found work, at Rostrevor, on the SS WOODLAND as an AB and he stayed with this steamer until the 23rd May 1915.

John Maginnis worked for Fishers of Newry for a short time after the war and he also skippered some fishing boats from Kilkeel Harbour. He was rightly praised for his seamanship when entering and leaving the harbour. He died in 1936 and is buried in Kilkeel Parish Church graveyard.

My Grandfather, Robert Charles Maginnis, returned to Kilkeel Harbour during the war and sailed on the ALPHA schooner with his brother 'Jimsey'. He fished for many years on the WATER LILY and other fishing boats. Robert Charles exchanged many a happy banter with his colleagues, John Ferguson and Willie Cousins while mending nets on the dockside. He lived with his wife Mary Jane and family on the Harbour Road. He died on the 24th September 1964 and is buried in the family grave in Kilkeel Parish Church.

The KILCOAN shipwreck lies on the seabed 18 miles NW of the Liverpool Bar Lightship at approximately 53.54 N 03.46 W. The ship is broken up from the bows to the boiler room with the cargo of coal strewn across the site.

Half-Model of KILCOAN (courtesy of Mr Trevor Scott, Kelly's)

Headstone of Robert Charles Maginnis
Kilkeel Parish Graveyard

SOURCES OF INFORMATION

I am grateful for the help given to me by the following people, friends, organisations and written sources.

1 Frank and John Maginnis, Kilkeel

2 Glynis and Royan Norton, Belfast

3 Jenny Caldwell, Larne Museum

4 Larne Borough Council

5 Larne Library Staff, Pound Street, Larne

6 National Archives, Kew, London. ADM 137/1057; BT 99/3140

7 Norman Whitla, Artist Kilcoan Painting

8 Howdens, Bank Road, Larne. Mr Stewart Rainey

9 Kelly's, Seal Road, Dargan, Belfast.
Mr Trevor Scott (Kilcoan Half Model)

10 'The Fighting Tramps –The Merchant Navy Goes to War.'
by Bernard Edwards (Hale)

11 'Business in Great Waters: U-Boat Wars 1916-45'
by John Terraine (Leo Cooper London)

12 'British Vessels Lost at Sea1914-1918.'
HMSO 1919 (Reprint 1977)

13 'Steam Coasters and Short Sea Traders'
by C.V. Waine & R. S. Fenton. Waine Research

14 Naval History Homepage World War 1
The Merchant Navy Volume 2 by Archibald Hurd

S.S.
DOWNSHIRE

THE SHIP THAT WAS SUNK TWICE

DUNDRUM

Dundrum village has a long and colourful history associated with its castle and Inner Bay Harbour. The castle erected by John de Courcy still dominates on a prime defensive site and the climb to the top of the keep rewards the tourist with a panoramic view over the village, the Inner Bay with its winding channels, the inlet, Murlough sand dunes and the outer bay area beyond the Bar.

The castle on the village hill has always interested me since it had an association with various Magennis chieftains but it has changed hands many times since 1601. It was the Sixth Marquis of Downshire in the late 18th century who started to have an impact on the village. Plans were drawn up to deepen the harbour and expand trade across the Irish Sea and beyond. Thought was given to the village infrastructure with plans for a hotel, lodging houses and parks. Spiritual needs were provided for the Methodists, Roman Catholics and Church of Ireland. The railway extended from Downpatrick in 1869 but unfortunately went through to Newcastle, which became the chief tourist magnet in South Down.

Downshire's legacy is still visible in the village and interested historians with a discerning eye are still able to pick out the relics of a bygone era. Dundrum has a rich heritage and there is a village trail with paths, picnic sites and parks for the visitor who has a mind to stand and stare. A paradise for the winter twitcher, summer fisherman and food gurus who like oysters and mussels.

The old Downshire Arms Hotel is still intact and close to the Bath House, which was part of the hotel complex. The Downshire Coat of Arms is clearly visible on both buildings. The railway line closed in 1950 but there are still traces near the quay on the northern exit from the village. The old track provides an easy stroll north along the side of the Inner bay. Another Downshire building, Murlough

House, is found further out in Murlough Nature Reserve with access gained by a long bridge across the Inner Bay.

Lord Downshire saw the potential of developing Dundrum as a seaport and in 1871 the East Downshire Steamship Company was formed. The quays were extended at great cost and streets were widened and new lines opened. The port became a busy place at the end of the 19th century and Downshire bought vessels, which brought timber from Canada and especially coals from England. Warehouses were built on the quayside to store grain and potatoes, which were the main exports. Coal, lime, cement, bricks, fireclay goods and Bangor Blue slates were common imports. One of the first ships purchased by the company was the SS LADY ALICE KENLIS built in Dumbarton in 1868. The company also owned the sailing barque RUBY, which was famous for crossing the Atlantic from Canada in 14 days.

Lord Downshire was a major shareholder in the company and some of his ships were named after members of the family, LADY DOWNSHIRE built 1873 at 240 tons and LADY ARTHUR HILL built 1885 at 271 tons. Three steamships were named DOWNSHIRE and two of these ships feature in this story. The first SS DOWNSHIRE was built in 1898 as a cargo steamer of 337 tons by the Ailsa Shipbuilding Company in Troon. She was a three masted vessel about 157 feet long by 24 feet wide and powered by a compound expansion engine, which gave her a top speed of 10 knots. 1903 was a typical year for this DOWNSHIRE and over the year she completed over 135 voyages. Destinations varied and the Dundrum steamer sailed to such places as Whitehaven and Liverpool. Also

Workington, Swansea, Neath, Warrenpoint, Maryport, Dundalk, Belfast, Irvine, Ellesmere Port, Preston, Ayr, Newry, Drogheda, Cardiff, Dublin, Ardrossan, Garston, Manchester and Troon. Cargoes were mostly coals, potatoes, granite setts, and also pig iron, breadstuffs, timber, iron ore, cattle and general cargo. William Henry Connor was born in the district of Ballylough near Castlewellan on the 15th December 1864. His parents were James and Julia Connor who were married on the 4th November 1863. Both his parents came from a farming background and James Connor's father was a carpenter by trade. Before he joined the SS DOWNSHIRE, William Henry Connor had gained a wealth of experience on a variety of steamers which took him to all corners of the globe. At 19 years of age, he served on the SS LADY DOWNSHIRE from Dundrum as a seaman in 1883/84 with Master Daniel Dove and other crew members that he would encounter later as Master of the DOWNSHIRE. He progressed to larger steamers in the 1890s such as the SS SOLWAY QUEEN, the SS CITY OF DORTMUND and the SS CITY OF LISBON. The latter ones were owned by P Murphy & Company of Dublin and provided him with the experience of working on much larger ships. When he gained his certificate, he returned to the East Downshire Steamship Company in the late 1890s. He married Margaret McNarry in April 1897 when he served on the SS CITY OF DORTMUND.

Captain Connor, in 1903, was supported by John Magowan as Mate, James McLean as 2nd Mate, Chief Engineer William Vance Marrs and Edward Torrens as Assistant Engineer. It was quite an eventful year with eight crewmembers being discharged and one fatality, Richard Hill a Fireman, born 1837 who died in an unfortunate accident at Whitehaven on 20th June 1903. This was a reminder to all the crew, that working on merchant ships was fraught with danger. Members of the crew had to be careful on duty and they rendered themselves liable to instant dismissal for drunkenness. The Captain was not immune to mistakes himself and he ran the ship aground in one incident while entering the harbour. The Log Book shows there was one deserter, William Gallagher, who had been a Newry Pilot in the past, had absconded at Garston on the 4th August 1903, after only 12 days service with the company. The Captain needed a reliable crew that he could depend on in times of crisis. A core of a dozen men stayed with the ship throughout 1903 and beyond.

All of the Downshire fleet had to navigate a difficult entrance into the Inner Bay. The bay was shaped like a hammer with a curving channel to the quayside. The Bar at Dundrum had about 15 feet of water at high tide and navigation was difficult at the best of times, given the 4-knot tidal current and the danger from maximum fetch waves powered by south east gales. The tidal range was high and at low tide the Inner bay was virtually empty except for the main channels associated with the rivers and tidal scour. Schooners and ships of shallow draught could enter with caution. It was best to enter at high tide but if the wind was from the southeast or east and gale force, there were many difficulties encountered as the waves were forced through the narrow breach in the sand dunes into the inner lagoon. The storm waves could break over the decks and there was a real chance that they could snuff out the boilers.

Dundrum Bay showing the narrow entrance

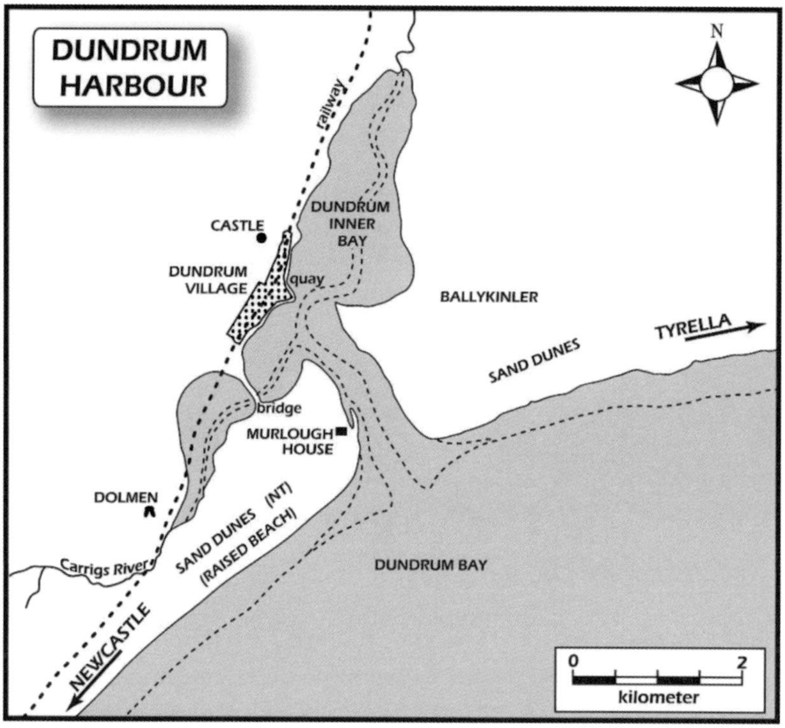

Tidal currents in the inner and outer bay areas were additional haz-ards.

A Downshire vessel came to grief in 1954 when she went ashore and lost a rudder. It is interesting to note that at the time of writing this chapter in 2012, there is a 'shipwreck' directly in front of the quay which fronts the stylish modern apartment blocks.

Dundrum harbour declined because of the tidal range problem, windblown sand and the development of bigger ships and bigger harbours at Warrenpoint and Belfast. There are only small pleasure craft and fishing boats in the Inner Bay today.

I was told a story over forty years ago about a German tourist who stopped in a Dundrum pub and said that he had been a submarine commander during World War Two. He said that he had sailed his U-Boat into the Inner Bay and out again at night. On the 20th February 1915, the U-Boats were not inside the bay but waiting outside in the wider expanse of the Irish Sea. The U21 had shown them the way and others followed Otto Hersing's lead.

DEPARTURE

At 2.00 pm on Saturday 20th February 1915, the SS DOWNSHIRE left the harbour on the high tide. She was steaming light with a load of 106 bundles of empty cement bags destined for Ellesmere Port on the Mersey. She intended to pick up a cargo of coal and sundries and return to Dundrum.

Most of the crew were from Dundrum except for the skipper who was now resident at 37, Glenmore Street, Albertbridge Road, Belfast and the Chief Officer, Thomas Turnbull who was from the Isle of Man. The steamer was licensed to carry steerage passengers but on this occasion, there were none on board. In such cases where passengers were permitted on board, the Board of Trade regulations post Titanic disaster, ensured that lifeboats were provided to a higher standard than normal steamer small boats. The two lifeboats on board were capable of carrying 40 people each and were well maintained by the DOWNSHIRE crew.

SS DOWNSHIRE CREW LIST 20th February 1915

1	Captain William H. Connor	Belfast	Master
2	Thomas Turnbull	Isle of Man	Chief Officer
3	John Connor	Dundrum	Second Officer
4	John Mullan	Dundrum	Chief Engineer
5	James Erikson	Dundrum	2nd Engineer
6	William Magowan	Dundrum	Able Seaman
7	Henry Murphy	Dundrum	Able Seaman
8	Alexander Morrison	Dundrum	Ord. Seaman
9	James Cardwell	Dundrum	Fireman
10	T. Carlisle	Dundrum	Fireman
11	William Martin	Dundrum	Steward

The Managing Director of the East Downshire Steamship Company was Edward George Henesey who lived in Dundrum. William Magowan and James Cardwell had served the company before, in 1901, on board the Steam Schooner DOWNSHIRE (66 tons). Mr Henesey was a driving force in the company and he was known as a hard taskmaster. As Manager of the company, he was concerned not only with the steamers and their cargoes but also the sawmill and the daily routines at the harbour. The latter tasks included looking after the lighting, the dredging, the levelling of quay berths and the Bar and River buoys. He was both feared and respected in equal measure by employees and showed an interest in the welfare of the village, especially educational achievement.

Chicken Rock Lighthouse near the Calf of Man

The SS DOWNSHIRE headed for the Chickens near the Calf of Man and the weather was favourable, being fine and clear with a light wind. Daylight was beginning to fade and Captain Connor was well aware of the submarine menace since he had been sailing across the Irish Sea on the day the U21 attacked on the 30th January.

THE SUBMARINE

Shortly after 5.15 pm when the ship was off the Chickens, a submarine was spotted two miles off abeam on the port side. Connor asked John Mullan, the

Chief Engineer, for full steam ahead and the stokers went into action providing extra steam in an effort to outrun the U-Boat.

This sub had a superior speed of 15 knots on the surface and she had already seen action that day further east towards the North Wales coast. At 11.30 am the SS CAMBANK, 3,112 tons, and owned by the Merivale Shipping Company Ltd of Cardiff was heading for Liverpool (Garston) with a load of valuable copper ingots and sulphur ore consigned to the Rio Tinto Company of Liverpool. She sailed from Huelva in Spain on the 6th February 1915 and faced gale force winds six days later when heading north. By the 14th February, the winds reached hurricane force from the North West and the heavy seas and pounding waves struck the ship on the port side, staving in the No. 1 hatch. She headed into Falmouth for emergency repairs and resumed her northward voyage on the 17th February. When she was five miles off Amlweh (Anglesey) with a Liverpool Pilot on board, Captain Thomas Richard Prescott of the CAMBANK and Mr Pass, the Pilot, saw the periscope of the submarine 300 yards away on the port beam and the track of a torpedo heading their way. Evasive action was taken by putting the helm hard a port, but it was too late and the torpedo hit the engine room on the port side. There was a terrific explosion with smoke and water everywhere. The 3rd Engineer and two Firemen were killed below deck and the vessel started to sink immediately. The funnel toppled and within eight minutes she buckled in the centre and went down. There was only time to launch one lifeboat on the starboard side and in the blind panic, Donkeyman Quigley from Glasgow missed his footing and drowned. One of the other victims was Michael Lynch, a Fireman, from Newry. Only 21 out of 25 safely escaped before the ship disappeared below the waves. They rowed away from the scene for a long time and were cold, wet and hungry before rescue came in the shape of the Bull Bay lifeboat, the JAMES CULLEN. A patrol boat, the armed yacht ORIANA followed and towed the lifeboat and ship's boat into Amlweh where the villagers gave the survivors a warm reception.

The QUEEN WILHELMINA liner witnessed this sinking and managed to outrun the U-Boat by going full steam ahead and heading for shallow water near Puffin Island. There was a suspicion in one report that German spies in Huelva had tipped off the German Navy about the cargo and destination of the SS CAMBANK. This submarine was now stalking the SS DOWNSHIRE.

THE ATTACK

The DOWNSHIRE had a top speed of 10 knots and the U-Boat steadily gained in the chase. Connor tried to change to a northerly course to avoid a torpedo attack, but the U-Boat was faster and tried to stop him with a shell from the deck gun fired from a quarter of a mile away. The DOWNSHIRE ignored this and sped on but a second shot was fired from a closer range. The chase ensued for about 25 minutes and Connor finally relented after a third shot landed close to the steamer. He decided to heave to lest his ship and crew were sent to the bottom. The engine room staff were allowed on deck and the entire crew assembled to await their fate, which was now in the hands of the submarine. They were now stopped about 8 or 9 miles northwest of the Calf of Man.

The submarine approached cautiously from 50 yards away with guns trained on the DOWNSHIRE and crew. The U-Boat commander spoke perfect English and hailed the steamer crew, ordering them to:

"Put out your boats and get into them."

They were also ordered to bring the ship's papers to the submarine. Connor obeyed these instructions and the lifeboats were made ready.

The U-Boat commander became irritated by the exhaust steam blowing off and bellowed:

"Stop that steam from blowing!"

The Chief Engineer was sent below to reduce the temperature and pump out the boiler to prevent the steam escaping through the waste steam pipe. When he came back on deck the rest of the crew were already boarding the lifeboats.

They had been given 10 minutes to rustle up their belongings and there was a mad scramble to pick up essential items such as food, water and warm clothing.

Captain Connor at the helm with his parrot

ON THE SUBMARINE

The two lifeboats were rowed to the submarine and Captain Connor was ushered on board. "Come this way," he was told along with three of his boat's crew. The skipper had a cocker spaniel, the ship's pet, and when he climbed on board the submarine the little dog followed his master. The German commander put five of his ratings into Connor's lifeboat and ordered two of the crew of the DOWNSHIRE (the Second Officer and Steward) to row them back to their ship. They carried a bomb in a brass canister, which was carefully lowered into the water amidships. There was a long fuse attached to this bomb and it was manoeuvred into position under the ship using a rope from the forecastle head of the steamer.

The Chief Engineer counted nineteen men standing on the deck of the sub armed with revolvers and swords. The deck gun was a constant threat. The crew of the DOWNSHIRE had difficulty in identifying the number of the U-Boat and the Second Engineer thought he had seen a No.12 on the stern. The Chief Engineer, John Mullan, said that some of the crew got into conversation with the German officers. "I thought you would hardly trouble about a little boat like ours?" A German replied, "You should not have made war on Germany." The Chief Officer reminded him that he had passed a number of fishing smacks and they had been untouched. To this he responded: "We don't interfere with fishing boats." "But why interfere with a light ship like ours?" The reply was much the same, as before: "You should not have made war on us."

When the fuse to the bomb was lit; there was a rumbling noise and the steamer began to sink headfirst. Her stern stuck straight up and she disappeared in two minutes just after 6.00 pm. When the boarding party returned to the submarine, the DOWNSHIRE sailors were told to row clear and "Take your little dog with you." The German officers were very courteous but clinical at all times. One of the officers said he was sorry they had to sink the ship, adding, "War is War." A common refrain in the sinking of merchant ships in the First World War. One report suggests that the German boarding party plundered the steamer for provisions.

The DOWNSHIRE crew in the two large lifeboats rowed towards two trawlers in the distance. There were six men in one boat and five in the other. The submarine forged away to the north and then decided to alter course. It soon disappeared into the darkness.

After half an hour's rowing, they were picked up by the steam drifters KIPPER and GOLDEN NEWS from Lowestoft. They were well looked after by the fishermen who had witnessed the whole incident. Each drifter took a lifeboat in tow and they reached Dundrum Bar by 10.00 pm. An hour's rowing brought them to Dundrum harbour at 11.00 pm where Captain Connor relayed the bad news to his manager, Mr E. G. Henesey and to the local Customs Officer. They raised the alarm about the U-Boat and advised other ports and the Navy about the danger.

***Captain Connor's Interview*.**

From an Interview in the Northern Whig 22nd February 1915.

> A machine gun on the submarine was trained on my bridge and was kept there during the time we were engaged launching our boats, a man standing by it the while. Our crew, numbering eleven, got into the two boats. Four of us went on board the submarine and taking our lifeboat five of the submarine crew got aboard the Downshire. Three men took an explosive with them, which they attached to our vessel. I was asked for the papers of my ship but all I gave them was her register.
> The questions I was asked were: "What port did you leave?"
> "Where are you going?" "Who are the owners of your vessel?"
> When the members of the submarine's crew returned with our boat we left. We had proceeded half a mile in our two lifeboats when there was an explosion and, looking back, we saw the Downshire going down bow first. As soon as our vessel went under the submarine moved off in a northerly direction and was soon lost to view. After going a mile and a half from where our vessel had been sunk we were picked up by two trawlers and were towed to Dundrum Bar. On the way one of the painters snapped with the result that we lost a boat, which I suppose, will be found drifting.

AFTERMATH

There was some debate about the identity of the U-Boat and the U12 or U21 were put forward as likely candidates. On 13th March 1915, it was reported that the DOWNSHIRE had been avenged by the British destroyer ARIEL. The ARIEL had rammed and sunk the U12 on Wednesday 10th March 1915 off Fife Ness. Of her 28 crew, only 10 were saved. This was the wrong submarine and we

now know that that the U-Boat involved in the sinking of the CAMBANK and the DOWNSHIRE on that day was the U30. The U30 was a member of IV Flotilla in 1914/15 and her commander was Erich von Rosenberg-Grusczyski. The U30 had been built in Danzig in 1912 and launched in 1913. During the war, the U30 sank 28 ships and surrendered on the 22nd November 1918. It was broken up in Blyth in 1919 - 1920.
Messrs John Atkinson & Co., 72, High Street, Belfast covered the war risk on the hull of the SS DOWNSHIRE. Shipping insurance was more difficult to negotiate because of the U21 attacks and, with more ships being lost to the U-Boat, premiums continued to soar. Despite the above insurance, Hansard Records show that on 10th March 1915, a Mr Bridgeman asked the President of the Board of Trade if the owners of the DOWNSHIRE steamship were to receive any financial assistance from the Government. A reply from a Mr Runciman stated: "As the DOWNSHIRE was not insured against war risks under the Government Insurance Scheme, it will not, I am afraid be possible for the Government to entertain any claim in respect of the loss of the vessel."

An armchair sailor at the Admiralty speculated that as the DOWNSHIRE was in deep water and 15 miles from Peel, it was in a favourable position for ramming the submarine. However, the vessel was small and light and no advice had been given on this subject to the crew. The shallow draught would probably have saved her from a torpedo and some skippers would probably have risked an attempt. This was easy to say from the safety of an office and I am sure Captain Connor put the lives of his crew first since he was clearly outnumbered and outgunned. He moved on to join the John Kelly fleet in March 1915 as Master of the SS KELPIE. This was followed by a short spell on the SS COMBER before he settled as Master of the SS CLANDEBOYE, in the latter half of 1915. This Kelly coal boat contributed to the war effort as a Royal Navy Collier from 1915 until 1919.

SS CLANDEBOYE

In 1925, Captain Connor was 61 years of age and living on the Albertbridge Road in Belfast. He had acted as Master of this ship for the last ten years. On the 13th April 1925, the coal boat left Ayr for Sligo and ran into a ferocious N.W. gale with winds over 60 mph. Captain Connor fought the storm over the next two days on the bridge as he saw this as his duty. By the night of the 15thApril, he was completely exhausted but insisted on doing his shift at the helm. At 9.30pm, he remarked on the state of the weather but refused assistance from the Mate, Daniel Kane from Islandmagee and his son, W. H. Connor. He stayed on the bridge, saying that 'the bridge was his place in dirty weather.' By 10.20pm, his devotion to duty and sheer exhaustion were just too much to bear and he dropped dead at the helm from heart failure when the ship was west of Tory Island. The Mate turned the ship around and returned to Belfast by the 17th of April and landed the body of the brave captain.

His son left the ship at the same time and Captain William Henry Connor was buried in Dundonald Cemetery on the 20th April.

THE SHIP THAT WAS SUNK TWICE!

In 1916, the East Downshire Steamship Company bought another steamship, built in 1905 by Mackie and Thomson of Govan for a Glasgow company. The ship was originally called the SS DUNSFORD when she was a workhorse for the Ford Shipping Company. She was rigged as a three masted schooner of 142 feet in length and 24 feet wide. Her name was changed to DOWNSHIRE when she was registered to the Dundrum Company in Belfast. E.G. Henesey in Dundrum again managed the new DOWNSHIRE in 1917. The Master, at this time was Archibald Harvey, 33 years old from 37, London Road, Belfast (between the Woodstock and Ravenhill Road). He was proud of his Australian origins and he was aided by experienced crewmembers from Dundrum & Newcastle.

SS DOWNSHIRE Crew List September 1918

1	Archi Harvey	Age 34	Adelaide	Master
2	James Kane	Age 45?	Islandmagee	Mate
3	John Connor	Age 36	Dundrum	2nd Mate
4	James Ward	Age 24	Dundrum	Able Seaman
5	Henry Murphy	Age 38	Newcastle	Able Seaman
6	Thomas Murphy	Age 24	Newcastle	Able Seaman
7	John Mullen	Age 54	Belfast	1st Engineer
8	James Cardwell	Age 39	Dundrum	2nd Engineer
9	Thomas Moore	Age 32	Glasgow	Fireman
10	John Cummings	Age 41	Dundrum	Fireman
11	John Brown	Age 18	Belfast	Boy
12	Benedict Gilmour	Age 30	Maryport	Royal Navy Reserve 1st Gunner
13	Alexander Souter	Age?	Lossiemouth	2nd Gunner

*Messrs Robert McConnell, 30 from Newry, William Thomas Price, 22 from Sheringham & somebody named Fagan? were discharged before the 21st September 1918.

After what happened to the first DOWNSHIRE, the ship's Log Book shows regular lifeboat drills and checking of life saving appliances. These drills mostly took place in Dundrum Inner Bay, but the Captain used the port or starboard lifeboat for trips ashore in the Mersey to look for orders. Despite this initiative the ship was often sailing light out of Dundrum, which was a sign of poor economics and intense competition. As part of the safety process the ship underwent a No. 3

Survey and repairs in Belfast from the 4th to the 20th September 1917. Voyages were to the usual destinations and mostly lasted one day, except for longer ones to Cardiff and then to Birkenhead. In the first half of 1917, the DOWNSHIRE completed 113 voyages and 102 in the second half of the year.
Unfortunately, from a business point of view, 97 or 45% of these voyages were light. On the 13th February 1918, there was a serious collision in the Garston Channel when the EMILY EVESON struck the port bow of the DOWNSHIRE causing serious damage.
This was the time of the unrestricted war around the British Isles and both sides were determined to maintain a blockade and starve each other into submission. This second steamer of 368 tons met the same fate as its predecessor on the Irish Sea shipping lanes. On the 21st September 1918, en route from Whitehaven to Dublin, with a load of coal she was pursued by the UB64 commanded by Oberleutnant Ernst Kreiger. I have been unable to find as much detail on this second attack because of the censorship requirements of the day and the fact that the novelty of reporting these sinkings had worn off since 1915. There were so many sinkings in 1917 that a lot of personal stories have now been lost. I found one Navy report on the incident and I include it here.

> Captured by submarine and sunk by gunfire. Vessel was owned by the East Downshire Company Dundrum. Left Whitehaven on 20th September 1918 for Dublin with a cargo of coal (350 tons) and 13 crew on board. Vessel was attacked at 12 noon and the steamer was then sunk by gunfire about 8 miles ESE of Rockabill, north of Howth. She sank at 2.00 pm.
>
> Attacked by gunfire from a submarine at about 4 miles distance, the ship's gun was outranged but the smoke defence was used with good effect. (The ship was armed with a 6 pounder.) After the ship had been hit twice, the master abandoned ship in two boats and the enemy was last seen firing into the ship. No lives were lost or men injured in the incident and the survivors were picked up by the SS SLATEFORD and landed at Dublin. Confidential papers were sunk by the Master.
>
> SS DOWNSHIRE

The change of name from DUNSFORD to DOWNSHIRE must have confused the German U-Boat commander. The Germans probably wondered why they had to sink the same boat twice!

It is surprising that there are not more stories circulating about the sinking of the two DOWNSHIRES in Dundrum and Newcastle. When you look at the crew lists, there appears to be 4 men, 3 from Dundrum and 1 from Newcastle, who served on both ships in 1915 and 1918. John Connor, John Mullen, James Cardwell and Henry Murphy must have witnessed both attacks and their stories have yet to be told.

After the sinking, Captain Archibald Harvey selected the same career path as Captain Connor. He joined the John Kelly fleet as a captain and served the company for 31 years. He had no problem with German U-Boats during the Second World War. He retired to his home in Carrickfergus in 1950, after serving on his last ship, the SS CARRICKMACROSS. He lived at 131 Larne Road, Eden, Carrickfergus when he died on the 16th June 1952. Archi was a member of the local branch of the British Legion and St. Patrick's Masonic Lodge. His funeral was attended by his sons and grandsons and took place in St. Nicholas' Churchyard, Carrickfergus with Canon J.C. Rutherford and Rev. T. Nolan officiating.

Captain William Henry Connor after the War

Sinking of SS DOWNSHIRE NO 2

CONCLUSION

There were no casualties in this sinking and it is interesting to note that the UB64 was commanded by Otto von Schrader in May 1918 when the Down fishing boats were attacked. The East Downshire Company bought other boats after this incident, first the SS MOUNT CHARLES, a smaller ship, and then another DOWNSHIRE in 1925. This was another Clyde built workhorse of 398 tons, 147 feet long and 24.6 feet wide built by Scotts Bowling Yard No. 297. She was a common sight on the seaways up to 1961, but she had a chequered history.

She saw service in the Second World War when captained by Harry MacCartney of Annalong. She carried arms to the Normandy beaches after the D-Day landings in 1944. The DOWNSHIRE was again dodging U-Boats as well as dive-bombers. She ran aground in Dundrum bay in 1954 and her cargo had to be offloaded on the beach before she could be re-floated. Boiler trouble was always a problem and she came to the end of her working life in 1961.

SS DOWNSHIRE at sea in 1925

The last coal boat to the quay at Dundrum was the BEN VARREY, a member of the Ramsey Steamship Company, which discharged its load of approximately 500 tons of coal on the 30th March 1984. East Downshire Ltd, which was part of the J. P. Corry Group, took the decision to end importing coal to Dundrum Quay because it was more cost effective to bring coal from Warrenpoint by lorry. This brought to an end the tradition established in 1871 by the Lord Downshire. There used to be 100 coal boats a year arriving in Dundrum but in 1984 the number had dropped to two or three per month and even less in the slack summer season. Lorries replaced the small merchant ships at Dundrum and ships of three to four times the tonnage of the Dundrum coal boats fed them. The law of economics led to the decline of this picturesque little port.

SOURCES OF INFORMATION

I am grateful for the help given to me by the following people, organisations and written sources.

1 Dr Royan Norton, Belfast

2 Kew Archives, London.
ADM 137/1057; ADM 137/2959; ADM 137/2964; BT 110/287; BT 99/3431

3 Downpatrick Heritage Library (Newspaper Library)

4 Central Library, Belfast

5 Public Record Office Northern Ireland, Titanic Quarter, Belfast
TRANS/2A/49/103A; TRANS/2A/49/103B; TRANS/2A/37/260A; TRANS/2A/37/260B

6 'Mourne Country' by E.E. Evans,
Dundalgan Press (W Tempest) Ltd 1967

7 'Steam Coasters and Short Sea Traders' 3rd Edition
by C.V. Waine & R. S. Fenton Waine Research

8 'Sailing Ships of Mourne'
Published by Mourne Observer

9 'Shipwreck Index of Ireland'
by R. Larn and B. Larn (Fairplay)

10 'Lecale - A Journey through Lecale'
by John Magee, Friar's Bush Press

11 SS DOWNSHIRE 1925 from Clydeside Shipbuilders Website
www.clydesite.co.uk Photo Donald Robinson

12 Ballymena Heritage Library – Newspaper archive (Larne Times)

13 Claude & Aileen Macquigg, Belfast 8 (2014)

Disused railway line en route to Dundrum

Dundrum Harbour 2013

A WOLF IN SHEEP'S CLOTHING

THE SINKING OF THE EDITH 27TH JUNE 1915

1915

The year 1915 was a bad year for the Mourne Men because the U-Boat war took a tragic turn with the sinking of the LUSITANIA off the Old Head of Kinsale on the 7th May 1915. This was a no warning attack on the Cunard liner by the U20 (Commander Walter Schweiger) that resulted in the loss of 1,198 lives out of 1,957 on board. Of the 785 passengers drowned, 124 were American and this loss of life swayed American public opinion and made them think again about joining the war effort on the side of the Allies. It is generally believed that a single torpedo struck the LUSITANIA, but a mysterious second explosion sent her to the bottom in 18 minutes. The cause of the second explosion has been a subject of debate since 1915 with many theories been offered. The wreck lies at a depth of 300 feet and one recent expedition in 2011 tested the merits of various materials, which may have caused the second explosion that occurred just after the torpedo strike.

The New York Times. EXTRA

LUSITANIA SUNK BY A SUBMARINE, PROBABLY 1,260 DEAD; TWICE TORPEDOED OFF IRISH COAST; SINKS IN 15 MINUTES; CAPT. TURNER SAVED, FROHMAN AND VANDERBILT MISSING; WASHINGTON BELIEVES THAT A GRAVE CRISIS IS AT HAND

Was it caused by a Coal Dust Explosion, Aluminium Powder, Munitions e.g. guncotton or a Boiler Rupture? Evidence suggested there were 4 million rounds of 303 cartridges on the manifest but little sign of illegal contraband munitions. The most likely cause was that the torpedo shot, 3 metres below the waterline, had been a freak shot that ruptured a boiler and resulted in the second explosion. Despite the disapproval of the Americans, the U-Boat campaign continued along the Southern and South West coasts of Ireland in June and July 1915. Stopping the trans-Atlantic trade with America was all part of the German blockade and the large merchant ships were still an easy target. The British merchantmen only gained some respite towards the end of the year due to the fact that there was a shortage of U-Boats on the sea routes to carry out their piracy.

THE ART OF DISGUISE

The U-Boat commanders were often deceived by British Q Ships, which had been encouraged by Churchill early in the war. In retaliation, they often adopted imaginative forms of deception to lure merchant ships into a false sense of security and thence to a watery grave. For example, the London steamer DIXIANA (3,329 tons) was sunk by the U41 on the 29th May 1915, 40 miles north of Ushant (West Brittany). She was on an Atlantic voyage from Savannah to Le Havre with cotton, pig iron for Swansea and some general cargo. The crew were allowed to abandon ship and floated in the channel for 24 hours before rescue by the Greek steamer SANOS SIFNIOS. The captain of the DIXIANA reported that the U41 had used sails to deceive them. Another U-Boat commander would use this method later in 1917 to dupe a Mourne schooner captain.

The U41 was later deceived itself by the Q Ship BARALONG and sunk by gunfire on the 24th September 1915. The latest German ruse had been countered by another act of deception and camouflage.

The U24 under the command of Rudolf Schneider off the Southern and South West coasts of Ireland adopted a more elaborate act of deception in June and July of 1915. Schneider had already had some degree of success when he sank the British battleship H.M.S. FORMIDABLE in January 1915 but it was a report from a schooner that would prove interesting. The Canadian registered schooner L C TOWER, was sunk by the U24 at 10.00 am on Thursday 1st July 1915, 25 miles SSW of Fastnet. The captain of the schooner reported that the U-Boat signalled 'Abandon Ship' and the crew left in their small boats. The schooner was subsequently bombed and burnt. The schooner captain observed the German crew rigging out the U-Boat as a steamer. Two dummy canvas funnels, two masts and a dummy bow and stern were apparently used. The piece de resistance was smoke coming from the funnels giving the impression of a heavily laden steamer instead of a deadly 65-metre-long attack submarine with 6 torpedoes and deck gun at the ready! The U24 was ready by 1.00 pm for another victim and headed North West while the crew in their small boats rowed towards Crookhaven and safety.

This disguise seems to have served Kapitänleutnant Schneider really well along the southern coasts and his war diary soon had a large catalogue of victims from the 27th June to the 1st July 1915 (see table below)

U24 Attacks

EDITH	Schooner	78 tons	British	27th June 1915
INDRANI	Steamer	3,640 tons	British	27th June 1915
LUCENA	Steamer	243 tons	British	27th June 1915
ARMENIAN	Steamer	8,825 tons	British	28th June 1915 29 casualties
DUMFRIESSHIRE	Sailing Vessel	2,622 tons	British	28th June 1915
SCOTTISH MONARCH	Steamer	5,043 tons	British	29th June 1915 15 casualties
THISTLEBANK	Barque	2,411 tons	Norwegian	30th June 1915
L C TOWER	Schooner	518 tons	Canadian	1st July 1915
SARDOMENE	Sailing Vessel	2,000 tons	Italian	1st July 1915
WELBURY	Steamer	3,591 tons	British	1st July 1915

THE EDITH SCHOONER

The EDITH schooner from Kilkeel must have been small fry to Schneider, but it was the workplace for three Kilkeel men. Thomas Doyle (age 43) was the Master with James Cunningham (Mate) and Thomas McDonald (Able Seaman) in support. (The latter was listed as Thomas McDollen in one crew list, but McDonald is more likely). The EDITH at 78 tons was steel built at Ulverston in 1876. She was registered in Barrow and, in 1915, was jointly owned by John Rooney and Thomas Doyle. Rooney was designated the Managing Owner and was living at the Royal Hotel, Kilkeel. They had bought the schooner from John McVea of Portavogie on the 22nd November 1913. On the 27th June 1915, the EDITH was nearing the completion of her voyage from Silloth (on the Solway coast north of Maryport) to Cork with a cargo of plaster of paris probably from the mines near Whitehaven. The U24 was waiting near Youghal, about 10 miles SE of Capel Island. Schneider used a simple deception this time. The steel grey submarine flew a Union Jack and showed no number. The captain was ordered to heave to and leave the schooner in 5 minutes as the enemy intended to blow her to pieces. Schneider saw this as an opportunity for target practice and, when the crew was 200 yards from the vessel, the U-Boat fired four shells into her hull and she sank just after midday at 12.10 pm. The three men from Kilkeel rowed towards Youghal and when near the Red Buoy, they were picked up by a motor pleasure boat owned by Dr Orpen of Youghal and they were towed into harbour by 4.00 pm. Dr Orpen brought the men to his residence, *MARINO*, and provided them with every comfort.

The yachting community in Youghal had heard gunfire in the distance and they feared another collier, possibly the LUCENA had been lost to shellfire by the U24. Captain Richard Evans reported that they had been fired on by the U-Boat and, after four shells the gunners found their range and hit the bow of the collier. They abandoned ship about 4 miles SE of Capel Island and took to the lifeboats

The EDITH in Kilkeel Harbour
(*Courtesy of the National Library of Ireland*)

after the U24 tried to request supplies of bread and water. Evans replied that he had no supplies on board and the deck gun fired another nine shells at the coal boat sending her to the bottom. A patrol boat picked up the crew from their lifeboats and landed them safely at Queenstown by 8.00 pm. Another steamer the KENMARE, owned by the City of Cork Steam Packet Company, successfully outran a U-Boat and reached her berth in Cork by 4.00 pm on the same date. At the time of these attacks, the legacy of the barbaric sinking of the LUSITANIA was still evident in the newspapers. Bodies, lifebelts and even a lifeboat were washed ashore on the southern beaches. The propaganda war rumbled on in the press and Board of Inquiry. It would be left to forensic marine archaeologists and conspiracy theorists to come up with a credible explanation for the second explosion. A significant number of the LUSITANIA crew who perished had come from the Newry and Warrenpoint area.

Schneider continued to seek out the merchant ships and transferred to the U87 in February 1917. In October 1917, he was washed overboard from the conning tower in heavy seas. Although a brave crewman rescued him, he died and was buried at sea after his short-lived career as a U-Boat commander.

THOMAS DOYLE and JOHN ROONEY

To find out more about the captain of the EDITH and the owner of this schooner, I paid a special visit to Kilkeel to talk to a renowned 'man of the sea', Gerry Doyle who lives within a stone's throw of the harbour. Gerry is a well-known fisherman with a bearded face lined with a lifetime's worth of stories and fishing lore. He skippered many fishing boats such as the EVENTIDE and the COREOPOLIS and he could tell many a tale about the harbour and dangerous crossings of the Irish Sea in search of sanctuary in a sheltered estuary.

He told me that he was related to Captain Thomas Doyle of the EDITH. Thomas Doyle was his grandfather Willie's brother. The captain's sister, Margaret Doyle, a milliner, was married to John Rooney, the owner of the EDITH, in 1897. He was a famous Kilkeel businessman who supposedly made his fortune in the goldfields of the Klondyke, hence his nickname 'Klondyke' Rooney. One theory suggests that he made his money elsewhere in America, in the copper mines of Montana and not the Klondyke. He was born in Moneydarragh near Annalong to parents John Rooney and Margaret Rooney (née McCourt) and went to sea at an early age on sailing ships. He struck lucky with his claim and was able to return to Kilkeel in the 1890s when he bought the Royal Hotel on Bridge Street from John Annett Junior and refurbished the rooms and interior in grand style. Apparently in his day, the hotel interior looked like something out of the 'Wild West'. He installed lighting and a fancy American style front with balcony and underhang. There was even a hitching post at the front and stables at the rear.

Kilkeel Royal Hotel building - now

Royal Hotel building - then

Rooney had the vision to see the potential for Mourne tourism more than a hundred years ago. Photos of the hotel show the name Royal Hotel and beside it in bigger signage the name Rooney's. In typical Kilkeel humour, the hotel was known as 'Wee Rooney's', which was not only a reference to his stature but also a mark of respect for his drive and ability to get things done. He used his capital to buy property, land, motorcars and schooners.

Politically he was a Nationalist from the old school and tolerant and progressive by nature. John Rooney was keen on improvements to Kilkeel Harbour in 1911 and he worked on a committee composed of local businessmen, fishermen, traders, boat owners and schooner men. Members present in Kilkeel Courthouse in November 1911 included Viscount Newry, Alexander Gordon JP, John Russell, James McKee, James Donnan, Thomas Chambers, John McBride, Thomas Edgar, John Davenport, Henry McBride, James Mackintosh and John Rooney. They formulated a plan to present to the Fisheries Branch that was part of the Department of Agriculture. Their plans for harbour improvement included a new dock, greater protection from storms, a deeper harbour, extension of the south pier seawards and an extension to the north pier, which would make it suitable for vehicular traffic and the landing of fish.

He quickly became a member of the Down County Council and, in 1913, he was in the cut and thrust of Council Meetings and Committees in Downpatrick and Rosemary Street in Belfast. Obviously as an elected member of the Council, Rooney would take a keen interest in Kilkeel affairs. He stood on the Committee for Agriculture and Technical Instruction (Fisheries Branch). Importantly, he was still a member of the Kilkeel Harbour Improvement Committee and responded to pleas for more space and improvement from local fishermen such as John Russell, who was concerned about damage to his boats lying in the river. Initially, he worked with Thomas Andrews from Comber, the father of Thomas Andrews, of TITANIC fame. Later, Colonel R.G. Sharman-Crawford D.L. from Crawfordsburn, North Down, replaced Andrews in the chair. Working with these people and the Rural District Council, Rooney was instrumental in getting a new harbour built for the lugger crews and a new road to the harbour, the Rooney Road, which is still named in his honour. He had one of the first motorcars in Mourne, like Dr Floyd another early motorist. Rooney owned a big white French Darracq, which he raced over the bridge and up Newry Street into the country roads, scattering the hoi polloi into the sheughs and ditches! Rooney built houses at the top of the Rooney Road and these were rented out to the local doctors, Dr Craig and Dr Hanna in the 1930s. He retained an interest in sea trade and, in 1915, he was registered as the managing owner of the EDITH.

Thomas Doyle sailed on the MILLBAY, a small ketch registered in Plymouth at 49 tons in 1880, after being built at Stonehouse. By 1902 this ketch had been bought by John Rooney of the Royal Hotel, Kilkeel and James Doyle acted as the Master. James Doyle was the Master of the MILLBAY right up to 1911.

Thomas Doyle sailed with him during this period. Later in 1914 he transferred to the EDITH when it was bought from John McVea in Portavogie. From February to April 1914, he approached the sail maker in Kilkeel and asked for the

topgallant, stay sail and boom jib to be made larger. This skilled work, by Captain Thomas Chambers, cost Thomas Doyle £4 15s 8d.
Thomas Doyle died young on the 2nd June 1918 possibly from stomach ulcers and heart problems, just after the sinking of the Kilkeel and Annalong fishing boats on the 30th May 1918. After the loss of the EDITH, Thomas Doyle and James Doyle (his brother) had 32 shares each in a new schooner called AGNES GLOVER. This schooner had been built at Tarleton, Lancashire in 1883 and was registered as 107 gross tons and 81 net. Her dimensions were typical of a schooner of the day at 87.5 by 21.4 by 9.8 feet. The brothers bought the boat as a replacement for the EDITH on the 8th December 1915 from the Isle of Man and she became a fixture in the harbour up to the time of Thomas's death at the age of 46 in 1918. Thomas also had a fishing boat, a smack with a lug sail and motor, called ALBERT. It was 33.5 feet long and had a gross tonnage of 6.47 tons. He used nets and lines for fishing and carried a crew of four men. This boat was transferred to James Doyle in 1918 and by 1939 it was the property of John Doyle, The Moor, Kilkeel. His brothers James Doyle, Albert Doyle and Henry Joseph Doyle and his two sisters Mrs Margaret Rooney and Mrs Minnie McGee survived Thomas Doyle. He bequeathed a half share of the schooner AGNES GLOVER to his brother Henry Joseph Doyle. The schooner was sold for £3,200 during probate.

John Rooney introduced the people of Kilkeel to the joys of the silver screen when he built a Picture Palace at the top of the Rooney Road in March 1919. This became a popular venue and, at Easter 1919, it was reported in the Newry Reporter that there was standing room only! This Rooney cinema could hold 300 and it originally showed silent films with Winnie Doyle providing a musical accompaniment on the piano. She also helped to change the reels on the projector. Mrs Rooney also took an interest in the picture house and by 1930 the talkies had come to Kilkeel thanks to the business enterprise of John Rooney. This little cinema was known as the Mourne in my day in the fifties and my brother and I, both Western fanatics, used to visit the first house in the Vogue and then race across the bridge for the second house in the Mourne. Thus, it was possible to see two Westerns on a Saturday night. I did not realise that it was thanks to John Rooney that I retained a lifetime's interest in the cinema.

Rooney also kept an interest in schooners and was no slouch on deck or at the helm. In 1917, he was registered as the owner of the BLACK CAT, a schooner built in 1869 and registered in Goole as 103 gross tons. The Master, at this time, was John Doran of Milestone House, Newry Road, Kilkeel. Records state that he was 25 years old and that he crewed with James Doran (55) Mate, Hugh Ferguson (40) AB (Able Seaman) and Willie McDonnell (27), all from Kilkeel. Voyages were mostly Dundalk to Garston and back again. Occasionally they headed south to Dublin and northeast to Glasgow. In the second half of 1917, there was one change to the crew and a young boy, Thomas Doyle (14), joined as cook from the Ferguson schooner JANE. In 1918, John Rooney and John Doran still operated the BLACK CAT and they were assisted by James Doran as Mate, Hugh Ferguson as an AB and Thomas Doyle as Cook. Later Daniel Kearney from Kilkeel and James Heaney from Annalong had spells on board. Rooney sold this schooner in the latter half of 1918. In 1923, Rooney had ownership of the schooner KATE that had come from Brixham. The KATE usually had four crew on board and courses were plotted to well-known destinations such as Garston, Cardiff, Glasgow and Port Madoc. John McKibbin (31) from Annalong, James Donnan (29) Kilkeel and Henry Joseph Doyle (38) Kilkeel had spells as the Master. Various people from Kilkeel crewed for them namely;

Patrick Curran (38) Mate	James Doyle (23) AB
Willie Curran (17) Cook	Tommy Donnan (25) Mate
Hugh Morgan (17) Cook	James Hogg (28) AB

John Rooney died suddenly when on holiday at Parkmore, Cushendall on the 19th June 1934. He was 73 years old and listed at this time as a wine and spirit merchant. He was still held in high esteem by townsfolk, especially the fishermen. His funeral was well attended and he was buried in Massforth cemetery. As a mark of respect at the harbour, black crepe was flown from the masts of luggers. The chief mourners at the funeral were listed as: Mrs Margaret Rooney (wife), Mrs P. Rodgers (sister), Mr P. Rooney (brother), Messrs Harry Doyle, P. Rodgers and Captain James Doyle (brothers-in-law), Mrs M. McGee (sister-in-law), Mr and Mrs James Doyle, Miss Annie Doyle, Mrs. Wilson, Mr. and Mrs John Rooney, Mr and Mrs Arthur Rooney, Mr and Mrs Fitzpatrick, Mrs Miller, Mrs Coyne (New York), Mrs R Codd, Miss K Rodgers (nephews and nieces), Messrs Willie and Hugh Rooney, Mr and Mrs Kinney and Mrs Murney (cousins) and Miss Lizzie Cunningham (friend). Kilkeel had lost a real character; he had some fortune in life and ploughed his money and ideas back into the Kilkeel economy.

THE ARMENIAN

In the list of vessels sunk by the U24, at the time of the attack on the EDITH, it is worth looking at the loss of the ARMENIAN in some detail, because it had a bearing on the course of the war at that time. Schneider seems to have extended his range well beyond his hunting ground around Fastnet and Youghal to sink this vessel. This ship was of interest to me because it had been built at Harland and Wolff in Belfast in 1895 at 8,825 gross tons. She was owned by the Leyland Line and, before the war, completed voyages between latitudes 70 N and 60S with Liverpool to Capetown a regular voyage. On the 28th June 1915, the ARMENIAN, which had been converted to carry animals for the war effort, was nearing the end of a trans-Atlantic voyage from Newport News to Avonmouth, with a cargo of 1414 mules on board being tended by a team of American muleteers. The mules were destined for the trenches and were essential, like the warhorses, for delivering supplies to the men on the front line. Captain Trickey of the ARMENIAN spied the U-Boat about three miles away and decided to try and outrun it using standard evading tactics. He was pursued for over an hour and subjected to vigorous and bloody fire from the U-Boat's 105 mm gun. The lifeboats had been swung out and several were damaged by shellfire. There were casualties on board as well, from the shrapnel. The steering gear was struck and knocked out of order. A shell went through the engine room skylight and one also destroyed the Marconi house. Another went down the funnel and disabled the stokehold. Thirteen of the crew were dead by this stage and the ship on fire in three places. The captain stopped the engines and the enemy allowed the survivors to take to the remaining lifeboats. Schneider rescued three men who fell from the boats. As soon as they were clear of the ship the U24 fired two torpedoes into the vessel sinking the boat, sadly with its cargo of mules. There were 29 dead, mostly American. The survivors bobbed around for 12 hours in the lifeboats and rafts before being rescued by a Belgian trawler called PRESIDENT STEVENS. They were eventually transferred to two torpedo boat destroyers and landed at Avonmouth on the 29th June 1915. Captain Trickey was awarded the Distinguished Service Cross for his efforts in trying to escape the U-Boat. The death of yet more Americans in 1915 caused a diplomatic ruckus and was another nudge towards war for the American President.

However, the Americans did not enter the war until 1917 despite the loss of life on the LUSITANIA and the ARMENIAN. The tipping point was the German declaration of unrestricted submarine warfare again on the 1st February 1917. The U.S.A. cut off diplomatic relations with Germany two days later. Final entry to the war was precipitated by another piece of deception by British Naval Intelligence. In January 1917, Naval Intelligence illegally intercepted a diplomatic cable on American territory. The German Foreign Secretary, Zimmermann, had sent this to the German Minister in Mexico.

The Zimmermann cable was diplomatic dynamite, because when it was decoded it said that if the U.S.A. came into the war on the side of the Allies, then Germany would propose an alliance with revolutionary Mexico and help the Mexicans reclaim Texas, New Mexico and Arizona. The source of the telegram was cleverly disguised by the British and passed on to President Wilson. The Zimmermann interception was instrumental in propelling America to war and they formally declared war against Germany on the 6th April 1917.

The EDITH was not the only Doyle sailing vessel sunk in the First World War. James Doyle had owned THE WHITE-HAIRED LASS, a ketch of 97/78 tons, in 1915. It had been built in Falmouth in 1885 and registered in Belfast. In May 1917, the ketch was sold to the Sarnia Shipping Company in Guernsey and sunk by the UB58 (Kplt. Werner Fürbinger) SSE (south-south-east) of Portland Bill when on a voyage from Cherbourg to Shoreham. There were no casualties and no loss of cargo as the ketch was in ballast.

The photograph of the U19 deck gun is a reminder of the role this German submarine played in Irish history in April 1916. Roger Casement had sought help from Berlin for the 1916 Rising and, 3 days before the rebellion on the 24th April 1916, he was returned to Irish shores on Banna Strand in Tralee Bay. The Germans had supplied some 20,000 rifles for the cause, but Casement thought this was not enough and wanted to postpone the rebellion. However, he was arrested when he reached dry land and executed for treason in August 1916. The 1916 Rebellion affected a lot of press coverage of the war in local newspapers and the attitudes of local people to German support, conscription, censorship and Home Rule. There were certainly spies and German sympathisers in Ireland, but how much information they fed to Berlin about troop movements, cross channel supplies and munitions is difficult to quantify.

SOURCES OF INFORMATION

I am grateful for the help given to me by the following people, friends, organisations and written sources.

1 'Shipwreck Index of Ireland'
by R. Larn and B. Larn, Fairplay

2 National Archives Kew. ADM 137/2959; BT 110/294/16

3 Public Record Office Northern Ireland (PRONI)
CUS/3/6/3/3; TRANS 2A/49/15A; TRANS 2A/49/15B

4 Down County Council 1917-18 PRONI LA3/50/A/2

5 Kilkeel Pier PRONI COM9/21

6 Northern Whig 28th June 1915

7 Irish Times 28th June 1915; 3rd July 1915; 19th July 1915

8 Newry Reporter Saturday 23rd June 1934 'Kilkeel in Mourning'

9 Families at Sea Project, Nautilus Centre, Kilkeel 2011

10 Gerry Doyle, Kilkeel

11 Fiona Jones, New Jersey

12 New York Times May 1915

13 Catherine Hudson, Kilkeel

U19 Deck Gun
Ward Park, Bangor

The U-Boat deck guns were often used to sink merchant ships.

KILKEEL, CO. DOWN.

Mountain and Sea Scenery. Ideal Roads for Motors and Cycles. Boating and Fishing.

The ROYAL HOTEL.

Commercial and Family.

Modern Up-to-date Garage. Cuisine and Wines perfect.

TARIFF.

Week Ends - - -	10/-
Bed and Breakfast, from - -	3/6
Boarding Terms, - - -	6/6

No Charge for Attendance.

JOHN ROONEY, Proprietor

n384

DOCTOR FLOYD'S WAR

FAMILY HISTORY

Dr Samuel Ferguson Floyd, as a Mourne Country Doctor and Surgeon before and during the First World War, was a true Mourne Man with an interest in many aspects of the community. He always had his finger on the pulse of Mourne, in more ways than one, and was privy to all parts of the circle of life from birth to the grave. He served Mourne as a medical practitioner for more than 50 years in local surgeries, peoples' homes and in the Mourne Hospital on Newry Street. He was on call for all emergencies, accidents, inquests and medical advancement. In his spare time, he showed a keen interest in new inventions and local ships. This chapter pays tribute to his work in the field of medicine at home and further afield on the battlefront. The roles of his only son, Hayden and wife, Mary are also relevant and are highlighted here.

At the time of writing in 2017, there are still people in Kilkeel who remember Dr Ferguson Floyd. Some worked with him in the hospital, some he had operated on and remembered the experience vividly and others remember him socially. He did not disclose much about his World War I experience to his friends and work colleagues and his descendants disappeared from Mourne. The last close relative, Everilda June Hughes, a granddaughter died in Australia on the 5th February 2009. Family records and Photo Albums may still be in Mourne and may surface one day when someone reads this tribute.

Dr Floyd was descended from Samuel Floyd of Kilkeel, a Greencastle Street Merchant in the 1830s. Samuel Floyd was a keen church goer and he was appointed a Church Warden in the Parish Church from 1841 – 1845. In business, he acted as a grocer and dealer in coal, spirits, coffee and tea. He also had a lime kiln at Mill Bay, supplied by limestone from County Louth on the other side of Carlingford Lough.

The Floyd family also had a Scutch Mill near Kilmorey Arms Square in 1845. The family home was near the mill and a tall chimney dominated the skyline with their shop nearby.

In 1845, Samuel Floyd was given the job of Registrar of Marriages for the District of Kilkeel. On 24th April 1845, the Presbyterian Meeting House of Mourne, (Magheramurphy Townland) was 'Registered for Solemnising Marriages therein.' Kilkeel 2nd Presbyterian Meeting House, as well as Annalong Presbyterian Meeting House and Ballymartin Congregational Meeting House were also registered for marriages. Samuel also dabbled in buying and selling property such as Needwood House and Farm near the Rectory in Kilkeel.

Samuel had four daughters, Margaret, Eliza, Jane and Ann. Margaret married Joseph May, a doctor and surgeon from Rathfriland and the other three married church ministers, two at least were Presbyterian.

Samuel's son, William, married Charlotte Hayden, one of six children born to the Rev. Henry and Mrs Jane Hayden. Mrs Hayden was the daughter of Alexander Chesney and Jane Wilson. They were married in Dublin, in the Parish Church of St. Peter with the Rev. G.A.F. Patton officiating. After their marriage, on the 10th August 1864, William and Charlotte Floyd had three children; Francis William Hayden, Samuel Ferguson and Joseph May Floyd. Francis died young as the result of an accident with a revolver, Joseph died in America in the 1950s and Ferguson (Fergus) remained in Kilkeel to fulfil his ambition to become a doctor. He was probably named after his grandfather or the poet Samuel Ferguson who was famous at the time. His work and poetry may have had an influence on Dr Floyd too, as the word *BORCHA*, the name of his final family home in the Square opposite the Kilmorey Arms Hotel in Kilkeel, appears in a poem by Samuel Ferguson about Mourne. In Irish, the spelling for Mourne is '*BOIRCHE*'. *BORCHA* was the name for a spirit herdsman of Ulster in the poem. *BEN BORCHA* referred to Slieve Bignian or it could be used to refer to Mourne Country.

I think Dr Floyd intended the latter reference when he called his house *BORCHA*, after all, he was to become the grand old master of Mourne Medicine.

MEDICAL STUDIES

William Floyd died at an early age of 40, after being inflicted with paralysis for his last two years as a Derryogue Farmer. He died at 'The Nest' on the Sand Road outside Kilkeel. Samuel Ferguson's interest in local boats may come from his father, who had experience of sailing a skiff. There is mention of him taking part in the Kilkeel Regatta on Thursday, 30th August 1855. The races commenced at 11am when 'a large concourse of spectators was assembled, including the local gentry, strangers from adjoining towns, a great number of elegantly dressed females, with the hardy stalwart peasants of the Kingdom of Mourne.' A brisk breeze sprung up and the first sailing match of skiffs began.

In 1st Place, was the ELIZA of Derryogue, owned by William Floyd and skippered by William Maginnis, second was the FANNY of Derryogue owned by Charles McBurney and skippered by John McCaver and third was the WAVE from Kilkeel, owned by Andrew Walmsley with James Campbell as skipper.

Next was a Yawl Race to the flag boat and back, a distance of 3 miles. First place went to the MARY of Derryogue, owned by Peter Kearney with William Maginnis again as Skipper, followed by the DEFIANCE of Derryogue owned by William McBurney and John McCaver in demand again as skipper. The Rowing Races followed these main events. It was heartening to read about the Derryogue boat successes as it was a reminder to me of Derryogue Harbour and its place in the maritime history of Mourne.

William Floyd continued the auctioneer tradition of his father and, in 1866, he started to sell off the Scutching Mill machinery - the Engine, Boiler, Handle Fittings and Rollers. He replaced his father as the Registrar for Marriages in the District of Kilkeel. He was also involved in letting houses and selling freehold property at auction in Mr Wood's Hotel in Kilkeel. When he died in 1874, he made provision in his will for the education of Francis and Fergus. Oddly, he specified in the will that they were to be brought up as members of the Presbyterian Church.

The family background ensured that Samuel Ferguson Floyd had enough money to pay for an extended period of training on the mainland, Belfast and Dublin. Fergus was educated initially in England at Christ's Hospital School, London and later, he followed his brother Joseph to the Royal Belfast Academical Institution (Inst) in Belfast. In 1887, Mrs Floyd was recorded as living at 62 Cavendish Street, Belfast and this dwelling must have been their base for their studies in Belfast. 1887 started badly for the Floyd family because of a shooting accident in Kilkeel. Francis William Hayden Floyd had returned home for the Christmas holidays from Belfast. He had been serving his apprenticeship in the establishment of Messrs. Barbour and Coombe Engineers. While trying to extract a bullet from a revolver, it accidently went off and entered his left breast and came out of his side. Despite assistance being given and attempts by the family to stop the bleeding, Dr Gordon was sent for and then Dr Wilson. Their efforts unfortunately did not save his life and he died on the 1st January 1887. He was only 18 years of age. Fergus had lost his father at an early age and now his elder brother. Another great loss followed when his mother passed away soon after the shooting incident in early 1888.

The Royal Belfast Academical Institution had a Medical School and students presented themselves for examination diplomas from the College of Surgeons, London; the Faculty of Physicians and Surgeons, Glasgow; the Apothecaries Hall, Dublin; the College of Surgeons in Ireland; and finally, for Medical Degrees at the University of London. Floyd studied medicine at Queen's College, Belfast from 1888 because it had an academic link to this famous school.

Dr Floyd's stethoscope

By November 1895, Floyd had taken his medical studies seriously and gained a wealth of professional qualifications. He gained so many qualifications after his name that he needed 8 letters of the alphabet! He had a Bachelor of Medicine (MB), Bachelor of Surgery (BCh), Bachelor of the Art of Obstetrics (BAO) and Licentiate of Midwifery (LM) from the Rotunda Hospital, Dublin.

Floyd's studies did not dampen his social life and, at some time, during his studies he met a certain Mary Hodgson from Belfast. She was the daughter of William and Mary Hodgson (née Fforde) from Belfast with an address at 2 Glenview, Springfield Road, Belfast. Her father was listed as an engineer or mechanic and he probably worked in one of the many mills in Belfast. Floyd had found his soulmate and the two were married in St. Matthew's Church of Ireland, Belfast on the 25th April 1895. They were to spend a long life together, right through two World Wars up to the 1960s. Hayden Floyd, their son was born in 1896 in Whiteabbey, Belfast. At this time, Fergus was probably serving his Houseman's year in Belfast. However, their family life was destined for Kilkeel and, unfortunately, it would be tinged by more family tragedy.

A MOURNE DOCTOR

It was only natural that Dr Floyd would return to Mourne Country since he had spent his formative years there. His parents had both passed away before he finished his studies. Charlotte, his mother, had died in Derryogue in 1888 at the farmhouse called 'The Nest' which was to become Samuel Perry's Farmhouse beside the Mitchell Farm next door. He had relatives and friends around Mourne, access to the sea and boats as well as a unique blend of mountain, plain and sea that he came to love and cherish during his working life.

Dr Floyd seems to have started off his Mourne medical career in Annalong Dispensary in 1897. Doctors charged fees in those days for their services and, sometimes when money was tight, payment was in the form of farm produce. Initially he made his calls by using a pony and trap. On treacherous winter nights, he had to be accompanied by a driver who looked after his pony while he attended to the patient indoors. He then changed to a motor bike or motorized tricycle in 1901, speeding up his service on a call out or emergency.

HIS MOTOR CAR

In the 1901 census, Dr Floyd and family are recorded as living in 16 Greencastle Street, Kilkeel. He was now 30 years old with 2 children, his son Hayden aged four and his daughter, Everilda May aged one. They all attended the Presbyterian Church across the road. There was also a 24-year-old servant in the house called Annie Collins and an 18-year-old nurse, Mary M^c^Intosh.

more than one occasion he had been called to a lugger, where a fisherman had taken a heart attack and died on the deck. One fatal collision off Kilkeel, I will relate in some detail because it affected many members of the fishing community, involved Dr Floyd at the Harbour and provided answers because there was an inquest.

THE MELISSA / ALICE COLLISION 1910

Dr Floyd and the good people of Kilkeel fishing community were involved and affected by this sea tragedy which occurred on Friday, the 16th September 1910. This was the time of year when the herring season was at its peak with more than three dozen fishing boats shooting their nets in the lucrative fishing ground to the south-east. The ALICE was not a local boat but she had sailed up from Arklow with Captain John Lynch in charge. The smack had arrived in Kilkeel Harbour on Friday morning with a decent catch of herring and went back out to sea again at 11.30 am. She was under sail, at 2-3 knots, and headed South East by East from Kilkeel Harbour towards the fishing grounds. It was a clear day with a visibility of 20 miles.

The John Kelly steamer, the SS MELISSA from Belfast, had left Dundalk at 10.30 am and Captain Irvine of Whitehead had plotted a course for Workington on the Cumberland coast, steaming at 10 knots. By 1 pm, tragedy struck in broad daylight about 4 miles out from Kilkeel Harbour when the steamer (560 tons) ran down the smack and sank her immediately. All seven of the ALICE crew were on deck, shouting at the steamer. As she bore down on the little smack, they shouted '***Murder! Murder! Are you going to run us down?***' They were struck amidships and almost cut in two. Three of the crew disappeared immediately. The other 4 crew struggled in the water and two men, Andrew Kelly (Arklow) and Jim Weddick (Balbriggan), clung to some wreckage, mostly from the stern of the smack. Captain John Lynch, the principal owner, swam around the wreckage before rescue by one of the steamer's lifeboats. Patrick

Doherty, aged 60 from Arklow, was also rescued but he was in an unconscious state. The four rescued men were taken to Kilkeel Harbour by the MELISSA and arrived at 2 pm. James Lynch (Arklow), Abraham Kearns (Arklow) and Jeremiah Lindsay (Wicklow) went down with their fishing boat.

Dr Floyd had been called in by the Coastguard who had seen signals from a vessel requiring surgical assistance. Word had spread around the harbour and crowds gathered on the pier waiting for the steamer to dock. Patrick Doherty's body was brought ashore and it was still warm. Dr Floyd tried for an hour to revive him but to no avail. He looked after the other three survivors as well. Andrew Kelly was badly injured and he was taken to Kilkeel Hospital where he was given further treatment by Dr Floyd.

The loss of life at sea on a clear day had moved the people of Kilkeel. Captain Lynch had not only lost his boat but also the sum of £108 in gold and notes in a bag which had gone down with his ship. Money was raised in Kilkeel for these men as well as a welcome change of clothing. Kilkeel fishermen made generous contributions to the fund on the 17th September 1910.

An inquest was held by the Coastguard on the same date where statements were taken from Captain Irvine and members of the crew. John Kelly arrived from Belfast and Dr Floyd had to attend to give the cause of Patrick Doherty's death. Questions were raised about lookouts on the steamer, but a full Board of Trade Inquiry had to wait until November 1910. This found the MELISSA at fault because the steamer did not keep out of the way of the sailboat and a good and proper lookout was not kept on the steamer. The Captain and Acting Mate should not have gone below to have lunch, leaving an inexperienced seaman at the helm, operating without a lookout and nobody else on the bridge to offer advice. The tragedy was a major topic of conversation in Kilkeel circles and some members of the gentry travelled to Dublin for the Inquiry which was well reported in local papers and in the Wicklow area.

Sadly, more tragic news was to follow the first inquest in Kilkeel. The smack, ALICE, had been named after Captain Lynch's daughter who was 22 years old.

When she heard news of the collision, she was overcome with grief on learning about the deaths of the crew. Her cousin, James, was one of the victims and she doubted that her father had survived. Support was given to her by a local doctor and church minister, but she was unable to cope with the strain and she passed away before her father returned. Captain Lynch now faced another ordeal and he left Kilkeel, on the 18th September 1910, to make a painful journey south to attend his beloved daughter's funeral in Arklow.

WAR

The 1911 census shows the Floyd family in residence at 21, Greencastle Street with 4 recorded in the large family house. The house was called *BORCHA* in the Kilkeel Street Directory. Fergus was now 41 years old and Hayden, an inquisitive teenager, at 14. Mary was 36 years old and helped, in her household duties, by a young servant called Bridget Boyle. The Floyds were now members of the Parish Church on Newry Street. Everilda May was not on the census and probably was in boarding school in Derbyshire.

When war was declared in August 1914, people in Mourne, like elsewhere, had challenging decisions to make about their future. There were political decisions for the Ulster Volunteers and Irish Volunteers, decisions about banks, food prices, recruiting, enlisting, fund raising, Empire or Home Rule. Soon there were Fund Raising Concerts in Kilkeel Courthouse and Dr Floyd's son, William Hayden Floyd, took part in a short play for the National Relief Fund, playing a Lieutenant in the Royal Navy. It was not long before he joined up for real. His father and mother also became involved, one in the local recruitment campaign and the other in collecting 'Comforts for our brave soldiers at the front' with the help of the Countess of Kilmorey.

Hayden Floyd was a mechanic by trade and a daredevil by nature. He joined up on the 19th October 1914 as a fresh faced 19-year-old in Belfast and decided to put his motor cycle knowledge and skills to effective use in in the Royal Engineers. He had his own motor cycle, a B.S.A. bought for £45 just before he enlisted. At nearly 5ft 9ins tall he was passed fit for service and then his bike had to be passed as well! He served as a despatch rider with the 5th Corps Signals and achieved the rank of Corporal (32239). At first, he trained in England until May 1915 and then moved to the front line in France. He was a member of the Royal Engineers Special Reserve (Motor Cyclist Section).

He saw action around Ypres, Loos and Neuve Chapelle. Despatch Riders were mainly used as couriers, delivering urgent messages and orders between HQ and the trench units. They were a vital avenue of communication where speed and secrecy were required. They had to be skilled cyclists as there was a lot of dodging shells and snipers as well as lorry transports supplying the front line. These riders did not often have the opportunity to 'scorch' along the roads and tracks to make deliveries because of the scourge of mud which slowed them down and created a daily clean-up. Hayden had to carry an extensive list of spares for his own machine such as a spare tube, tyre repair kit, plugs and magneto spare. As a mechanic by trade, he probably carried out his own maintenance on rest days. Other men from Kilkeel, like Andrew Mulholland and Jimmy Ross, were not very far away from him, but they were in different regiments.

Recruiting from the start was thought to be slow in Mourne but it was not long before the Recruiting Agents arrived in Kilkeel. William Johnson, a Newry solicitor, was particularly conscientious in his campaigns through Mourne. He could be over-zealous at times and, on one occasion, he ambushed a group of farmers after mass in Killowen and proceeded to visualise the consequences of a German landing on Carlingford shores and associated land grab! He made many visits to Kilkeel during the war years, mainly during the Fair Days. He was the Chairman of the Newry and District Recruiting Committee and, when he came to Kilkeel, he was helped in his endeavours by Dr Floyd, Alec Gordon JP and Mr Carey from Mourne Grange School.

Dr Floyd could not have failed to notice the arrival of the R.A.M.C. (110th Unit of the Royal Army Medical Corps) as they marched through Newry, Warrenpoint, Kilkeel, Annalong and Newcastle. They were followed by the Royal Irish Fusiliers and The Connaught Rangers. The bands would play and rousing speeches would be provided by Messrs. Floyd, Gordon, Carey, Johnson as well as spiritual input from the Rev. A. Eadie and, finally, patriotic tales from Regimental Lieutenants and Sergeant-Majors.

FRIENDS IN HIGH PLACES

The Floyds rubbed shoulders with many dignitaries of the day, especially in the Church and Arts. W.B. Yeats, Sir Hamilton Harty, Percy French, the Kilmoreys as well as fellow doctors, sea captains and boat builders were all close friends. Fergus was a skilled navigator and, along with the Earl of Kilmorey, sailed one of the Earl's fishing boats, the ELLEN CONSTANCE, from Lowestoft to Kilkeel.

Percy French, the song writer, poet, painter and entertainer was a regular visitor to *BORCHA* and, it was said that there was even a French Room in the house, reserved for his visits. In November 1951, when Mrs Mary Floyd was invited to the unveiling of a fountain in Newcastle, dedicated to the memory of Percy French, she recalled his visits to Kilkeel and Mourne Country.

Mrs Floyd said that she first encountered Percy French about 1910 as a member of the United Arts Club in St. Stephen's Green, Dublin. The friendship endured during his lifetime and Percy had an open invitation to stay at *BORCHA* when he was performing his recitals at Kilkeel Courthouse. Percy had as many as 23 summer concert venues around Ireland, performing his famous songs like 'Mountains of Mourne', 'Slattery's Mounted Fut' and 'Are Ye Right There Michael?' Seaside resorts such as Bangor, Newcastle and Portstewart needed entertainment in the evenings and provided a steady income for him until the war upset the tourist trade.

Usually, he informed the Floyds by express letter that he was on the way to their residence but, on occasions, he arrived unannounced in his bedroom upstairs with easel and paints in use and a tune taking shape in his head. Percy was a talented painter and produced many sketches, watercolours and oils of Irish Bogland. He was also adept at smoke paintings completed on stage. These were drawn on white plates using a candle and delicate strokes with a match produced a typical Irish scene, maybe a colleen leading a donkey down a lane. He sometimes used an acetylene lamp in the production of his unique smoke sketches. Mary Floyd said she kept a stock of cheap white plates, acquired on a Kilkeel Fair Day, in case Percy came to a dinner party and offered to do his party piece for the individual guests! Percy French had tales to tell about his travels around Ireland, his time on the railway and, more recently, entertaining troops on the Western Front in France.

Mary Floyd was conscious of the war and organised a War Hospital Supply Depot from *BORCHA* during the war to aid the Sick and Wounded at Home and Abroad. Fergus helped her with her charitable work throughout the war years.

Later in 1916, she would not be thinking of a dinner party but a Sphagnum Moss Party!

THE BOARD OF GUARDIANS

Dr Floyd sat on a lot of committees in Kilkeel and he was forward looking in terms of civic improvement for the population. This included a deputation to the Kilkeel Rural Council in support of electric light provision for the town. In educational enhancement, he was keen to establish a new Technical School for the younger generation because their choice was limited, mainly due to the lack of railway track between Newcastle and Warrenpoint. He had ample support from many men of influence like Robert Hanna, (General Merchant), Robert Boyd, John Rooney, Alex Gordon and many others prepared to put their case to the Down County Council.

Floyd was not only a Medical Officer for the Hospital but also an active member of the Board of Guardians set up to provide relief for the poor in the Workhouse nearby. The numbers during the war years could vary from 75 to 108. These numbers fluctuated daily, depending on the rate of discharge or death.

In 1914, John Haughian acted as Chairman with Alex Gordon, JP as Vice Chairman and Peter Murney as Deputy Vice Chairman. John O'Neill, retired sea captain from Killowen was another prominent member who had a lot in common with Floyd since his son had also joined up. The war had affected the price of medicines and supplies with a general increase and the Board of Guardians, on a tight budget, had to shop around. Decisions had to be made about the best coal and best price when orders were 100 tons a time.

The Workhouse had a Farm and the inmates did try to cut costs by producing hay, potatoes, oats and milk. They also bought and sold cows. Problems, some slight and others more serious, would arise daily e.g. a fire destroyed the Cow Shed and one ton of bedding straw; the Schoolmistress showed no genuine interest in teaching her charges; Scarlet Fever cases necessitated bringing in extra nurses from Belfast; the inmates complained about Indian meal being used for porridge and Coffins for the dead had to be bought in at 1s 4d per foot.

Floyd and the team of Guardians looked carefully at the running costs of the complex and sent out tenders to acquire the best deals on provisions, clothing, bedding, medicines, surgical instruments and burials. Patients required lockers in the Infirmary where costs could average 7s 4d per patient per week, this was 1 shilling more than a Workhouse inmate, at 1916 prices.

THE SPHAGNUM MOSS PARTY

The local gentry were very aware in 1916 about what was really happening on the front line and they were keen to do their bit to help the war effort in small but effective ways. In September 1916, there was a concerted effort to collect sphagnum moss in the Mournes, before winter set in. This followed another meeting in Kilkeel Courthouse under the leadership of the Countess of Kilmorey and other dignitaries; Dr Floyd, Dr Evans, John Russell, Rev. Dr McMordie, Rev. H. Martin and others. Samples of the precious moss were on display and they made arrangements for a large party to go to the Deer's Meadow to gather the moss. This is a well-known water catchment area and source for the River Bann which flows on a long journey north to reach the sea. On the other side of the watershed, the River Whitewater has a short journey to the sea. Today, visitors stop to admire the view of Spelga Dam or seek out the old bridge when the reservoir is low.

The moss was to be used for treating wounded soldiers because of its antiseptic properties. The Kilkeel group had to gather the moss and ensure that it was clear of all foreign matter, no heather or bits of stick. A depot was to be opened at the Red Cross Hostel, The Square, Kilkeel for receiving and inspecting the moss by the Voluntary Aid Detachment, before delivery to the War Hospital Supply Depot in Belfast. From there, it could be sent to the War Dressing Supply Depot in Edinburgh.

HAYDEN FLOYD AND THE ROYAL FLYING CORPS 1916

This was the year when everything would change in Floyd's life, and indeed for the people of Ireland. Hayden was still on the Front and making an impression. On the 18th March 1916, he was discharged from the Royal Engineers and obtained a commission in the Royal Flying Corps, 11 Squadron, as a 2nd Lieutenant. After training in the use of Lewis Guns and flying, he was assigned as an Observer in a flimsy biplane, an F.E. 2b (Farman Experimental 2).

This plane was powered by a Beardmore 6-cylinder piston engine and could reach speeds of 91mph. It was made of mostly wood and canvas which afforded no protection from the Fokker Scourge machine guns, prevalent at the time over the Somme. Hayden's plane usually had 2 Lewis Guns and he, as Observer, would sit in the nose of the nacelle with the Pilot behind him and slightly higher. There was a good field of fire forward but there was difficulty in

firing to the rear. You had to stand up and balance precariously to shoot backwards over the upper wing. This meant you had to avoid the Pilot and, especially the propeller, which was behind the wings! The sketch of the imagined dogfight shows how they might have fought in 1916. The disadvantage for Hayden Floyd was that the Fokker Eindecker in the drawing had a synchronised gun mount which meant that this enemy plane could fire through the propeller. The technology was so secret that the German Pilots were forbidden to fly over enemy lines in case the technology fell into British hands.

At the beginning of July 1916, the Battle of the Somme raged on many fronts with thousands of casualties. By the 9th July 2nd Lt. Hayden Floyd was acting as Observer with Pilot 2nd Lt. David Hamilton Macintyre. They were flying on an offensive patrol over the German lines when they were attacked by a Fokker plane. Hayden was severely wounded in the head and leg and the controls of his plane were badly damaged, causing it to crash land behind enemy lines near Baupaume. Hayden was taken to a German Field Hospital at Fevreuil where he died from his wounds on the 11th July 1916, aged twenty.

On Patrol, July 1916.

His Pilot survived uninjured and became a prisoner of war. He is quoted as saying: 'His death is a great blow to me; when he fell he asked me for a cigarette and gave me some chocolate. He fought with great courage and was the very best of fellows.' Hayden was buried by the Germans in Grave 80 at the Chateau of Fevreuil and later his remains were transferred to the British Cemetery at Douchy-La-Ayette.

Major F. O'Brien, Royal Flying Corps, reported 'the excellent duty performed by Hayden before he fell into the hands of the enemy'.

This was to be a terrible blow for the Floyd Family in Mourne but, like many other fatalities, the sad news was very slow to filter through the long lists of casualties from the Somme and elsewhere. Initially, it was reported that Hayden was a prisoner of war and, although badly wounded, he was 'progressing favourably'. This was all unofficial and the report of his death did not reach Kilkeel until the end of August. Fergus had lost his only son and he set off for the front to visit his grave. Details of this perilous journey are sparse but Fergus was a man of action and apparently, he went to France and the front line on board a rickety aircraft. I suspect that the Earl of Kilmorey, a close friend, helped him plan this sorrowful expedition. He found Hayden's grave in a war-torn wood and experienced the hell of the war from close quarters. Mary Floyd, racked by grief, went with him as far as London but did not travel to France. That journey would come later.

This family loss had an impact on Fergus and, by October, he planned a certain course of action which would take him to war using his medical skills. He told the Board of Guardians that he had joined the Royal Army Medical Corps (R.A.M.C.) and applied for six months' leave of absence to go to the front, where there was a dearth of doctors. He nominated as his substitute, Dr H.E. Evans, medical officer of the Kilkeel No. 2 Dispensary District. The application was unanimously granted as they understood his motivation. A vote of sympathy was also passed to him on the death of his only son, Hayden.

THE HOSPITAL SHIPS

Dr Floyd is recorded as joining the R.A.M.C. as a Temporary Lieutenant on the 15th November 1916 and he subsequently was assigned to a Hospital Ship. These ships were requisitioned by the Admiralty and were mostly former cruise ships or passenger ships. They were essential for the chain of evacuation of the wounded from the battlefront in France or Gallipoli to British Hospitals or new auxiliary hospitals, usually grand country houses loaned to the Red Cross or St. John's Ambulance Brigade for the duration of the war. The ships were fitted out as floating hospitals, former dining rooms and smoke rooms were converted into operating theatres and wards for hundreds of patients. By taking away partitions, cabins were changed into wards for as many as 900 patients. They were painted white with large red crosses on the hull, according to Hague Convention rules and sailed with lights on at night.

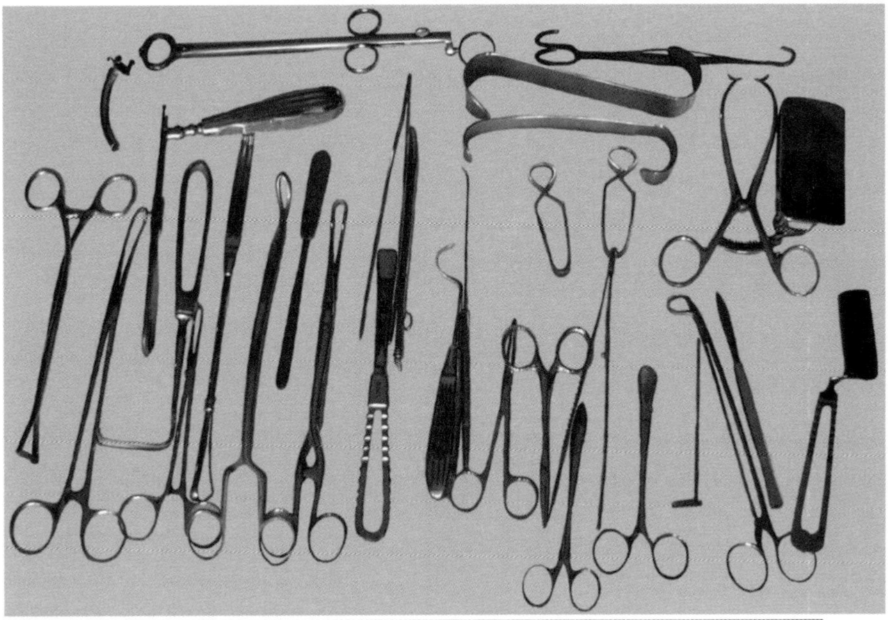

Selection of medical instruments
Courtesy of Dr A. Mitchell

Dr Floyd, while on board a hospital ship, had to learn quickly and make decisions instantly because there was such a wide range of injuries. He had surgical instruments (see photo), basins, tables and dressings. Most patients would have been classified in a Casualty Clearing Station with labels or pen markings on their forehead before sailing. Gas Victims were usually put in a special ward because a lot were blind and needed oxygen. Infection could set in at any time and a gangrene operation would then be necessary. An amputation could take as little as 15 minutes with chloroform and ether applied.

The surgeon in a gauze mask would proceed with morphia injections on standby and a Drug Box near an assistant nurse. He would then have to work quickly with a saw and scalpel, artery clips, artery needle, forceps and file for stripping the bone before the stitching of the stump and addition of the final bandages.

Fergus must have endured the full horror of war through his patients. Trench foot, bullet wounds, blast wounds, burns, mustard gas damage, shrapnel wounds, infections, tetanus and shell shock. He would have had to deal with members of the ship's crew as well. There were many ailments among the crew of a hospital ship and, on one ship I researched from Floyd's period of service, there were cases of diabetes, flu, abscess, bruises, dermatitis, venereal disease, neuritis, rib fractures and tonsillitis as well as suicide attempts.

The main problem for Dr Floyd during his brief stint in the R.A.M.C. was that the Germans decided to move the goalposts again. In late January 1917, as part of the renewal of their unrestricted submarine warfare, they declared that hospital ships of the Allies and Britain were employed for the purposes of transporting troops and military supplies as well as the wounded. Thus, hospital ships in the English Channel became soft targets and, as luck would have it, Dr Floyd's hospital ship was torpedoed.

Fergus gave an interview to the Mourne Observer in 1956 about his time in the R.A.M.C. This amounted to only one paragraph and in it he said 'his ship was torpedoed in the English Channel, but happily few lives were lost, and the crew was picked up by another ship within a matter of hours'. In another article in 1968, it was reported that he was on board a hospital ship which was torpedoed while returning from the Gallipoli Campaign. It is a frustrating point to make but I often wonder why reporters when interviewing members of the public who served on ships, do not ask the obvious question; 'What was the name of your ship?' In Dr Floyd's case, because he was a temporary recruit, his records were destroyed in the 1930s and there is now only one record left about the hospital ship he served on. There were two hospital ships that fitted into his time frame (November 1916 – May 1917) and both were torpedoed in the Channel with a comparatively low loss of life. H.M.H.S. ASTURIAS, built by Harland and Wolff in 1908 was one possibility and H.M.H.S. GLOUCESTER CASTLE, built in Glasgow in 1911 was another. There are other similarities. They both had a recent voyage to the Mediterranean to pick up the wounded from Salonika in Greece which would connect both ships to the Gallipoli Campaign. They both survived the torpedo attacks in March and were salvaged for future use. My best guess was that Floyd was on the GLOUCESTER CASTLE because it had the lowest loss of life, only 3 while ASTURIAS lost 35. Thanks to research carried out by Robert McIntosh, Curator, of the Museum of Military Medicine in October 2017, I received confirmation that Fergus was ranked as a Captain on the GLOUCESTER CASTLE from the 15th November 1916 until the torpedo attack in March 1917.

Both hospital ship attacks are worth mentioning because they are typical of the period and paint a heroic picture of the crews and R.A.M.C. Staff on board these vessels.

HMHS ASTURIAS

This ship was a Royal Mail Steam Packet Company ocean liner built in Belfast with a length of 520 feet, twin screws and a tonnage of 12,015. She was associated with the Southampton to Buenos Aires route before she was requisitioned by the Admiralty to serve as a hospital ship, decked out in white with a broad green band and large red crosses. As well as the required operating theatres and wards, there were radiology and disinfecting facilities installed. On the 30th November 1916, this vessel left Southampton to pick up the wounded in the Eastern Mediterranean. She stopped in Malta and then on to Salonika to evacuate casualties and return to Malta. By Christmas 1916, ASTURIAS returned to Salonika where she stayed for over a month. On the 27th

January 1917, she sailed for Toulon then back again to Salonika on the 24th February 1917. Twelve days later and carrying a 1,000 wounded, she headed back to Blighty via Malta. This voyage went well, and she arrived at Avonmouth near Bristol where the wounded were taken off. Captain Slater, R.A.M.C. signed off all the casualties as Senior Medical Officer on board.

Captain Charles Laws and Chief Officer Arnold Thompson set a course back to their familiar port of Southampton on the 20th March 1917. Near midnight (11.54 pm) and south of Start Point the ship was torpedoed by UC 66 (Oblt. Herbert Pustkuchen).

Captain Laws summarised the damage as follows: -

'The ship was hit aft on the starboard quarter by a torpedo wrecking the crew's quarters, disabling the ship and flooding the after holds and engine room. Several of the crew were killed by the effects of the explosion and an accident to the Port After boats, 35 in total'.

The torpedo destroyed one propeller, the rudder and the flooding meant there was a loss of control of the engines. The ship steamed on at 8-10 knots which resulted in a tragic loss of life when an attempt was made to launch a lifeboat. The explosion had broken containers of disinfectant which created fumes that killed at least one crew member. There was no real sense of panic on board and, although taking water, she sailed on and beached herself near Bolt Head providing a photo opportunity for the locals from Salcombe. Once beached and stationary, the lifeboats could be launched safely, and landfall reached.

A month later, the ship was successfully re-floated and taken to a dry dock in Plymouth. By this time, she had been bought by the Admiralty and served as an ammunition hulk for the rest of the war.

H.M.H.S. GLOUCESTER CASTLE

There were many similarities in the attack on this vessel which occurred on March 30th at almost the same time, 11.55 pm. A major destination for this hospital ship was again Salonika and she was berthed there in January 1917 when she helped evacuate the wounded, along with H.M.H.S. DOVER CASTLE. By mid – January, some of the wounded were discharged to hospital in Malta. Then, it was back to Southampton for the 7th March 1917 and a shorter route to Le Havre to pick up the wounded from the Clearing Stations in France. From there, patients were brought back to Southampton, offloaded and then back to Le Havre to pick up more. It was on the way back to Southampton on the night of 30th March that the ship was torpedoed by the UB 32 (Kplt. Max Viebeg), off the Isle of Wight.

GLOUCESTER CASTLE
(*Courtesy of Nautilus Centre*)

This hospital ship had been built originally for the Union Castle Line and commissioned as a 410 Bed Hospital Ship on the 24th September 1914. At the time of the attack, there were 399 casualties on board, some were German. 300 patients were classified as cot cases (stretcher cases). The fact that all the wounded were successfully removed on the night of 30th/31st March by the crew and R.A.M.C. staff is a credit to the organisation of the Master Edward John Holl, Chief Officer John Watson-Black, Chief Engineer Harry Black, Captains Tierney and Floyd of the R.A.M.C. and the ship's Matron, Alice Alana Cashin from Australia.

The Master's report of the torpedo attack was written in detail and gives an excellent account of what happened on board. The torpedo exploded at 11.55 pm on the starboard side and the blast caused flooding in the engine room and stokehold. The aerial core parted, rendering W.T. (Wireless Transmission) useless and all electric lights went out. Orders were given at once for assembly at Boat Stations and patients were organised and made ready for the lifeboats by the R.A.M.C. staff. The nurses had to remove all wooden splints from fractured legs, in case the patient ended up in the sea and the splinted leg became buoyant. This was likely to force the patient to lie on his back and increase the risk of drowning. Rockets were fired continuously until assistance arrived. About 12.30 am, a small steamer, SS KARNAK, arrived and orders were given to lower away the lee boats. This vessel was owned by the Moss Steamship Company of Liverpool and Master Charles Ruthven Stewart was in charge. Ladders and ropes were already lowered in preparation for the rescue. The steamer proceeded to take the wounded on board from the lifeboats. The crew used a cane basket, slung from one of the ship's davits, to lift the cot cases on board. This was a tricky operation because of the heavy sea but all were safely rescued, thanks to the sterling efforts of the crew. Two lifeboats were also salvaged, as an insurance policy in case there was a further torpedo attack. Matron Cashin ended up on this ship and was praised for her calm and orderly conduct during the evacuation procedure.

There was no panic on board the hospital ship and most had slept with clothes on, just in case the ship was torpedoed. Every patient had a lifebelt on and the number of a lifeboat station. A well-organised evacuation procedure was in place and the crew and patients waited calmly for the other rescue ships which were not very far away.

Next to arrive was Destroyer P19 (Escort Vessel), commanded by Lt. J.B. Colvin, on the lee quarter. More boats were lowered and ordered to row round leeward to the destroyer. Colvin started to rescue patients from the lifeboats and they were carefully crammed on board P19. Shortly before this first destroyer was filled with 350 patients, Destroyer BEAVER appeared and hailed the hospital ship. This ship had a radio that worked and naval command was made aware of the U-Boat attack on the hospital ship. Colvin advised Lt. Quinn, on this bigger destroyer, to go alongside the hospital ship and take off the remaining patients, doctors, nurses and crew. Captain Fergus Floyd was probably one of the 30 R.A.M.C. staff rescued by the BEAVER crew at this stage of the evacuation. Again, this was carried out in an efficient manner and patients were lowered to the decks of the destroyer with the expectation of warm blankets and hot coffee. Over 100 were safely transferred.

The Carpenter, then produced some good news and reported to Master Holl that the ship was still dry both ends and only taking water in No. 3 Hold, besides the Engine Room and Stokehold. The Master decided to remain on board with a few volunteers and he sent his crew to join the BEAVER. It was now about 2 am and Lt. Quinn ordered all rescue vessels to extinguish their lights in case the U-Boat returned to fire another torpedo. This destroyer stood off and promised to stand by the crippled ship. P19 and KARNAK were ordered to Portsmouth, but the Moss Line steamer stayed until 4.30 am and took more survivors on board.

BEAVER signalled at 4 am that she would try to tow the ship to shallow water. On the first attempt, the hawser parted. Lt. Quinn then headed for Portsmouth with Dr Fergus Floyd on board. Destroyer HORNET arrived later at noon and again tried a tow, but the hawser parted a second time. Two tugs hove into sight and saved the ship by hooking their hawsers to the bow. They commenced towing and successfully beached the ship in Stokes Bay where she lay grounded in 6 fathoms of water. The Port Anchor was dropped, and, thanks to a valiant rescue operation, the ship was ready for salvage. It was towed back to Southampton a fortnight later and repaired.

The Chief Engineer on the GLOUCESTER CASTLE reported that 3 crew were missing, Alexander Lamb, 4th Engineer and Greasers, William Williams and Henry White. They had been on watch in the Engine Room at the time of the explosion. Their bodies were recovered from the Engine Room, after the water had been pumped out from the ship on the 20th April. Their remains were immediately removed to the mortuary and the cause of death was given as drowning. The bodies were handed over to relatives for burial.

The patients were taken by the rescue vessels to Portsmouth Milton Hospital. Fergus then spent the remainder of his war on another hospital ship, named H.M.H.S. AQUITANIA. This was originally built as a Cunard Ocean Liner with a 45,647 gt, 10 decks and a length of 901 feet. It was the last surviving 4 funnelled liner from the same stable as the R.M.S. MAURETANIA and R.M.S. LUSITANIA. She played many roles in the First World War, first as an armed merchant cruiser, troopship, hospital ship serving the Dardanelles campaign and then back to service as a troopship. When Fergus arrived at Portsmouth she had returned to her hospital ship livery and she was laid up in the Solent. He may have even lived on board this large vessel until he relinquished his commission on the 14th May 1917 and returned to his duties in Mourne.

The attacks on the hospital ships were answered by a reprisal bombing raid on a German town. A large squadron of British and French planes carried out a bombardment of Freiburg, S.W. Germany on Saturday the 14th April 1917. The aircraft attacked a crowded city centre from French airfields which were close to the target. People were killed, buildings destroyed, and leaflets dropped to explain the reason for the revenge bombing raid. Freiburg suffered at least 25 Allied air raids during the war.

Master Edward John Holl of the GLOUCESTER CASTLE was awarded the Distinguished Service Cross in 1917 in recognition of his contribution to the war effort. He transferred to another Union Castle transport, SS LEASOWE CASTLE, which acted as a troopship for the Admiralty in the Mediterranean Sea theatre of operations. Master Holl was always diligent on his ship and keen to prepare for every eventuality, especially U-Boat torpedoes. He tried to ensure that his crew could launch lifeboats, row, sail and use sea anchors. This was a wise precaution because, on the 20th April 1917, he was torpedoed again near

Gibraltar by the top German ace, Lothar von Arnaud de la Perière in the U35. He managed to limp to port and the ship was repaired. There were no casualties.

However, on the 27th May 1918, at 12.25 am when in convoy from Alexandria to Marseilles, he was torpedoed again by UB51. There were 2,903 troops on board and Holl plus his Chief Officer put their evacuation procedure into operation. There were two rescue craft nearby and the captain was determined to launch all boats and save as many troops as possible. About 100 men were lost in this attack. Captain Holl never thought about his own safety and unfortunately, he went down with his ship when it sank rapidly at 2 am. He was awarded the Board of Trade Gallantry Medal (Silver) for his devotion to duty which was presented to his eldest son in 1919.

BACK TO WORK

Fergus returned to Kilkeel and continued his high work rate. In his absence, he had been appointed to the Select Vestry of his church and he had to catch up with the Board of Guardians as well. There was a debate about using part of the Workhouse as premises for a new Intermediate School. Fergus was in favour of using the disused part for a Technical School. On a more mundane level, several inmates had managed to escape down Newry street to the pubs and came back intoxicated. On one occasion, the police had to be called in to sort out the drunks and the doctors to sort out the injuries.

They were still conscious of the war in the Workhouse Kitchen and an effort was made to collect fruit stones and nut shells for urgent war purposes. This collection was related to the use of gas warfare and the issue of gas masks with charcoal filters to combat the effects of gas. Towards the end of the war, it was realised that a more effective filter could be made from charcoal that came from burning fruit stones and nutshells. The Workhouse Kitchen became a source of raw material and perhaps Dr Floyd encouraged the collection because he saw the effects of gas warfare on board the hospital ship.

V.C. HANNA COMES TO TOWN

This was one of the biggest public events in Kilkeel during the war and Fergus was closely involved in the organisation and planning of the presentation in front of Kilkeel Courthouse. Robert Hanna had emigrated to Canada in the early 1900s where he worked as a farmer and a logger. Originally from Aughnahoory, Kilkeel, he joined the Canadian Expeditionary Force and became a Company Sergeant Major in the Canadian Infantry (29th Battalion Vancouver). He was awarded the Victoria Cross for his courage and leadership in storming a German machine gun position near Lens in France. With bayonet and rifle butt, he neutralised four German soldiers and secured and held the position until relief arrived. The people of Mourne, from all sections of the community, decided to mark Robert Hanna's return to his parents and Mourne with something special. A sturdy platform was constructed in front of the Courthouse and bunting and flags were hung round the square. The band of the Royal Irish Rifles from Newry played lively tunes and by 3 pm, thousands of people had gathered to see their own Mourne Hero and man of the moment. The modest hero arrived by car with his parents and awaited to be 'lionised' by the local clergy and gentry.

Fergus read the address which featured scenes of Hanna's home, Kilkeel Harbour, his Regimental Badge and the Victoria Cross. He praised the courage of the recipient and then he called on Thomas Hanna, a Crimean veteran wearing his two medals from an older war, to make the presentation of the address and a wallet of Treasury notes donated by the people of Mourne. Robert Hanna rose to give thanks and was greeted by loud cheers from the thousands of people who had gathered in the square. He said he was pleased to be back in Mourne and thanked all for the illuminated address and generous gift – whatever it was he did not know! This produced a cacophony of laughter and applause. Modest to the end, he said that 'many other soldiers had done as brave and braver deeds than he had done, but they unfortunately had not been heard of since'. He had 'done his duty' just like Sergeant Hanna who had helped to capture Russian guns to earn his medals. This must have been a poignant occasion for Fergus to witness because Hanna was a son who survived and came back.

Bottom left: Dr Floyd, Sgt Hanna & VC Hanna
Taken February 1918
Photograph courtesy of the British Legion, Kilkeel

THE END OF THE WAR

Numbers in the Workhouse had dropped towards the end of the war and by 1919 there were only 16 inmates. There was talk of closure and transfer of the poor from Kilkeel to Newry Union. After the end of the war, there was another tragic inquest for Fergus to investigate on the 20th November 1918 in the

Workhouse. This was the death of an infant caused by asphyxia from convulsions or having been overlain by the mother. The flu epidemic of the time was also a serious problem for the doctors, as this strain killed 100 million worldwide.

By 1921, Mary and Fergus had their daughter's marriage to plan and host in Kilkeel. Everilda married Richard Pierce Hughes in early March 1921 and then moved to Kensington in London.

A new doctor arrived in the practice in the 1920s and Fergus acted as his mentor. Dr Billy Hanna was to become a well-respected Mourne Family Doctor with a reputation as a keen gardener at his house, *PACKELOT* in Ballyardle. Fergus showed him the procedures in the Mourne Hospital and out in the field on emergency visits. They communicated by telegram, in the early days, with simple messages and codes. For example, 'Come Quick' followed by the address of the patient. They had their motor car, their doctor's bag and a travelling kit dispensary, in case a prescription was necessary. Emergencies at a farm might have resulted in the use of a kitchen table as a makeshift operating table. There were cases where chloroform and ether were needed to anaesthetise a patient, a strangulated hernia for example. Caution was called for, where open fires were lit, as these gases made a lethal explosive mixture; a case of brown trousers during the hasty operation. Other emergencies might include a tonsil operation and Dr Floyd was a dab hand at using his little guillotine! There were also cases where the two men dealt with pregnancies, miscarriage complications, appendicitis and pleural tap operations using a stab incision and a trocar. Floyd was a skilled role model for Dr Hanna and the latter, I remember well with Dr Craig at the Rooney Road Surgery in the 1950s.

Fergus kept up his interest in boats and he would take his grandchildren out in his motorised skiff for a sail. The Kilmorey girls were also keen sailors and Fergus would venture as far as the Isle of Man on some occasions. He was also friendly with the Mackintosh Brothers at Kilkeel Harbour. As renowned boatbuilders, Fergus was often invited to attend sea trials on one of their new boats at the harbour.

Mary and Fergus were regular travellers abroad, especially on cruise ships across the Atlantic, or to North Spain (Santander) and down under to Melbourne, Australia with P&O on the SS STRATHAIRD. The latter voyage occurred in November 1951, after he had been awarded an M.B.E. for his long service as a doctor in Kilkeel Hospital. The King made the presentation in mid-February 1951 at Buckingham Palace. Fergus was now 81 years old and this was an occasion to treasure. His friends and work colleagues honoured the occasion by hanging a portrait and citation near the entrance to the hospital for many years until its closure. Sadly, this historic building disappeared to make way for a new housing development in 2016.

Dr Floyd's M.B.E.citation
(Courtesy of Dr A. Mitchell)

There was one final tragedy inflicted on the family in 1953 which was completely unexpected. A grandson, Hayden Floyd (Peter) Hughes M.A. who was close to his grandparents in Kilkeel, had been living with his father at 37,

Addison Road, London. A bright boy who had studied at Mourne Grange, Kilkeel, Charter House, England and went on to graduate from Cambridge University. He used to drive Fergus around Mourne on his rounds and he was planning to return to *BORCHA* as his sister, Mrs June Campbell, had recently arrived from Australia. He was studying for his final degree in architecture in London when he was killed in a gas explosion after trying to light a gas fire in his study. He was cremated in London and his ashes were brought back for interment in Kilkeel Parish Church.

MEMORIES

In their twilight years, Mary and Fergus continued to be involved in Kilkeel affairs. Fergus was a key member of the British Legion (Vice President), with the Earl of Kilmorey (President) and he took the salute on Remembrance Sunday in November 1960. Mary loved her garden flowers, especially snowdrops and relaxed indoors with her extensive book collection. Always gracious and tolerant with a quiet sense of duty, she continued working for the community in charity work and taking up Chairmanships when needed. Dr Floyd's eyesight had been failing since the 1950s and Mary would read to him constantly in *BORCHA* which they strived to maintain and improve. Brian Mulholland wrote to me from Australia about the time he and his brother, Michael, plastered all the ceilings for Doctor Floyd in the 1950s. Brian said that Fergus had poor eyesight at the time and, fastidious by nature, they had to lift him up onto a table and then onto a chair, so he could rub his hands on the ceiling to check for smoothness. He was a formidable doctor to younger patients, gruff at times on committees and abrupt on occasions because he did not suffer fools gladly. To his close friends, he was a gentle and caring person who appreciated a high work ethic, acquired from the Victorian era. He maintained his link with the hospital until the end and Sister Maureen McKeown, who was Matron there for 8 years, remembers him walking up to visit his colleagues, dressed often in plus fours, flat cap with pinch-nez glasses for close inspection. Mary would drive up later to collect him.

Mary predeceased him and passed away on the 1st March 1963. Fergus died 5 years later, on the 16th September 1968 at 98 years of age. The Rev. James Mehaffey officiated at both funerals in Kilkeel Parish Church. British Legion Honours were accorded Dr Floyd at his funeral and members dropped poppies on his coffin at the close of the committal. The Rector paid tribute to a man of sterling character, great courage, strong faith and dedication to his profession in Mourne. The funerals were well attended by members of the medical profession associated with the Mourne Hospital and local surgeries. They are both buried in Kilkeel Parish Church on Newry Street and are still remembered as people who made a difference by the older generation.

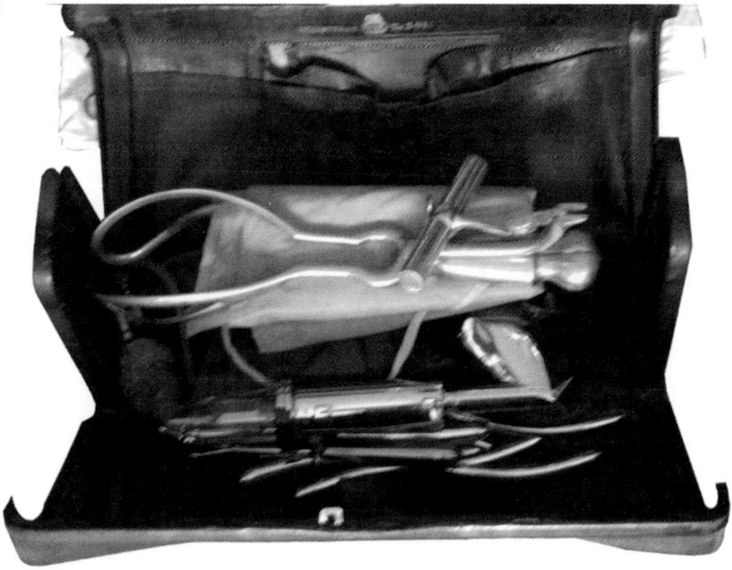

Contents of a doctor's Medical Bag

(*Courtesy of Dr A. Mitchell*)

SOURCES OF INFORMATION

I am very grateful for the help given to me by the following people, friends, organisations and written sources.

1 Mrs H.A. Maginnis, Family Historian, Bangor

2 Dr Arthur Mitchell, Retired Mourne Doctor, Kilkeel

3 Sister Maureen McKeown, Kilkeel

4 Trevor Graham, British Legion, Kilkeel

5 Maureen & Brian Mulholland, Australia

6 Staff in Belfast Central Library & Newspaper Library

7 PRONI - Dr Floyd's Will, 5th Dec.1968
Kilkeel Board of Guardians - Minutes BG/16/A/92

8 The National Archives Kew
BT 165/1528 - GLOUCESTER CASTLE 1916
BT 165/1712 - GLOUCESTER CASTLE 1917
BT 165/1683 – ASTURIAS 1917

9 Mourne Observer
3rd November 1951 - Newcastle Memorial to Percy French
14th March 1953 - Death of Grandson
22nd June 1956 - The Floyds of Kilkeel
8th March 1963 - Mary Floyd
20th September 1968 - Dr S.F. Floyd, M.B.E.

10 Outlook Newspaper
17th January 1964
14th January 1966 (Photo)
28th June 1968

11 Belfast Newsletter
16th Nov. 1910; 5th May 1914; 28th Oct. 1914; 29th May 1915.
8th Oct. 1915; 15th June 1916; 22nd Aug. 1916; 30th Aug.1916.
9th Sept.1916. j 31st Oct. 1916. k 29th Dec.1916 l 24th April 1917;
20th Aug. 1917; 5th Feb. 1918; 28th Feb. 1918

12 Newry Reporter - Saturday 2nd March 1918 (V.C. Hanna)

13 London Gazette - 11th Dec. 1916 & 5th July 1917 (Dr Floyd)

14 Northern Whig - 15th Feb. 1951 Dr Floyd, M.B.E.

15 'A Directory of Ulster Doctors' - Vol.1 (2013)
Compiled by R.S.J. Clarke (U.H.F.)

16 Royal Belfast Academical Institute, Belfast (R.B.A.I.)
Peter Anderson, Director of Development, 2017.

17 R.B.A.I. Centenary Volume 1810 – 1910. J.H. Robb

18 u boat.net - U-Boats WW1.

19 findmypast - Passenger Lists.

20 Mourne and the Great War
Schomberg Festival Committee, Kilkeel

21 'Newry & Mourne in the First World War'
An Education Resource 2015 Newry and Mourne Museum Education Service. (Dr Robert Whan, Museum Staff and Volunteers)

22 Robert McIntosh MA AMA Curator
The Museum of Military Medicine, Aldershot

23 'The War on Hospital Ships 1914 – 1918' by S McGreal
Pen & Sword 2008

Special thanks to Dr Arthur Mitchell of Ballyardle who knew Dr Floyd. He provided me with a wealth of medical detail, amusing stories and numerous artefacts and photos which help illustrate this chapter. I enjoyed his story telling, poetry, eye for detail and love for Mourne Country.

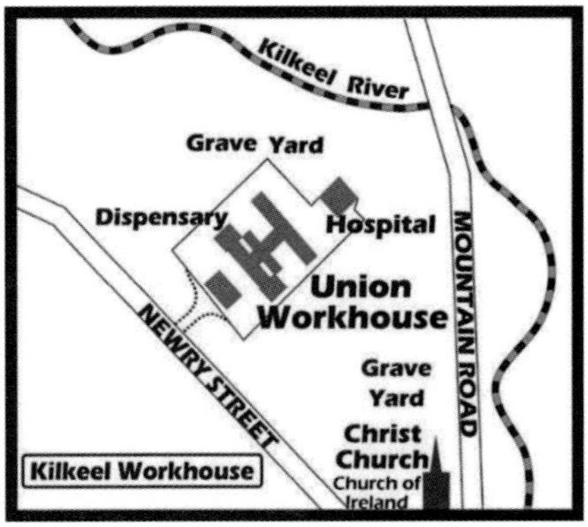

VERILDA MAY HUGHES
JULY 3 1901 — SEPT 27 1932
HAYDEN F. HUGHES M.A.
FLOYD
MARY FLOYD
MARCH 1 1953
S. FERGUSON FLOYD

CAPTAIN JAMES FERGUSON
KILKEEL SCHOONER MAN

A TALE OF A SUBMARINE, SHIPWRECK, BAD LUCK AND SURVIVAL

Alan Crozier of Warrenpoint often visited his aunt's guesthouse on the Harbour Road in Kilkeel when he was a young boy in the 1950's. He became fascinated by a pair of binoculars that were displayed in the kitchen. There they were sitting on a dresser, small, well used with a flash of brass giving them their own air of reverence. They were a major attraction for a young lad wanting to view Slieve Bignian in the distance. He could also use them for spotting buses coming down the Harbour Road loaded with guests for Harbour House. His job was to alert his Aunt Marian about the arrival of the buses so that a warm welcome could be prepared for the tourists. The binoculars remained a source of mystery for years until his Aunt Marian, the youngest daughter of Captain James Ferguson, told him the story behind their origin.

Harbour House, Kilkeel

MAY 1917

In May 1917, World War 1 was raging on many fronts on land, sea and air. In Belfast, you could still go to the cinema to see Mary Pickford or Douglas Fairbanks. People awaited the arrival of D.W. Griffith's epic 'Birth of a Nation'.

Variety acts on stage were brought over at great expense from London. Agricultural shows took place in a rural setting and marching preparations were being made for the Twelfth. The papers of the day set a different tone and they devoted a lot of column inches to the frontline battles and the associated lists of casualties and awards for bravery. In government, the two main issues of the day were HOME RULE and the SUBMARINE MENACE. Lloyd George and Edward Carson were under pressure to grapple with and solve both problems. Some newspapers in London had created a sense of panic about German U-Boats and their daily cull of merchant navy ships. Carson was trying to reorganise the Admiralty to deal with the U-Boat menace. Ingenious plans were being thought up to stop the shipping and trawler losses; such as the Trawler Section, Q Ships, Sea Plane Patrols and fast sleek destroyers armed with 'ash cans' (depth charges) to protect the convoys. One British Submarine, the C15 (which features later in the story) was involved in an unusual experiment to use sea lions to track submarines! This was all part of the Admiralty's Board of Invention and Research but unfortunately the sea lions were inconsistent in their pursuits and were prone to distraction by the local fish population. Please don't ask about the plans for using seagulls!!

CAPTAIN JAMES FERGUSON

Captain James Ferguson lived on the Harbour Road with his wife Mary Ann from Ballinran townland, his son Robert James, daughters Isabella, Margaret and Marian. He was well trained in the art of sail, having come from a seafaring family. He learned the ropes from an early age and could trim a sail to maintain a steady six knots along the seaways and later use a topsail brake to enter a narrow harbour. His schooners and ketches traded the Irish Sea routes between Scotland and Merseyside. He knew these routes off by heart and he often relied on his brothers Hugh and John to crew for him. When the wind was in his favour, he could cross the Irish Sea in 12 to 14 hours but other times the voyage could take a week, because of head winds.

The 'JANE' painted by James Ferguson

In his lifetime, he owned, or part owned a series of sailing ships such as GUILD MAYOR; LADY LILFORD; EARNEST; JANE; MARIAN and the HENRIETTA. He frequently worked with Captain James McKee in buying and selling fishing boats and sailing ships. They both relied upon trade in granite and potatoes outbound and coal inbound. James McKee was an established coal merchant

Captain James McKee

in Kilkeel and was also involved in buying and selling fish. They were associated with other ships such as: AMELIA JANE; GIPSY; KILTIE; ELLIE PARK; MARTHA ANN; and WIZARD. Coal brought in by Captain Ferguson was often distributed directly from the hold to local farm carts, which had been invited in by Captain James McKee.

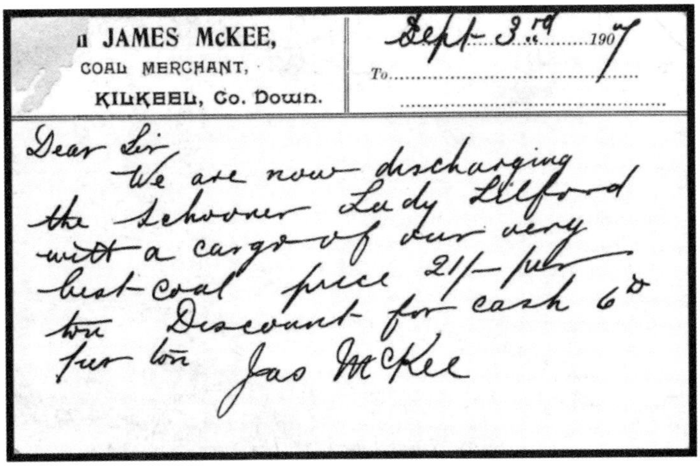

JAMES McKEE,
COAL MERCHANT,
KILKEEL, Co. Down.

Sept 3rd 1907
To.......

Dear Sir,
We are now discharging the Schooner Lady Ilford with a cargo of our very best coal price 21/- per ton Discount for cash 6d per ton Jas McKee

Postcard from James McKee to John Millar, Derryogue farmer

Captain Ferguson was small in stature (about 5ft 6ins) and neither smoked or pulled a cork. He was well respected in the town and carried an air of authority and dignity associated with a tough schooner captain who did not like slackers on board his vessels. He sported a moustache and wore a cap when at the helm. He spent his entire life based at Kilkeel Harbour and he made his living from trade and buying and selling shares in sailing ships. He was ambidextrous and produced fine paintings of his schooners in his free time. He could complete the detailed brushwork involved with his left or right hand.

THE SUBMARINE

On the night of 2nd May 1917, Captain James Ferguson was beating his way south in his schooner the EARNEST on the Ardrossan to Dublin route with a load of coal on board. The EARNEST was a three masted schooner of 111/90 tons built in 1884 at Tarleton (Lancashire), owned by James McKee and James Ferguson. They had 32 shares each in this schooner, which had been bought from George Gray and Benjamin Swanson from Orkney. (Benjamin Swanson sold 32 shares to James McKee and 12 shares to James Ferguson. The other 20 shares came from George Gray and were sold to James Ferguson on the 5th July 1916.)

The crew of EARNEST were all Kilkeel men and were listed as Master James Ferguson age 44, Joseph Ferguson age 36, William John McBride age 30 and Francis Curran age 18. The Managing Owner, James McKee of Fairview House recorded that the crew had joined the ship on the 1st January 1917.

On this calm spring morning, the EARNEST was trying to find enough wind to belly the sails as it slowly headed south past Skullmartin near Ballywalter, keeping well away from the dangers of North Rocks and South Rocks. Unfortunately, Ferguson did not realise that another hazard was lurking in the morning light. There was a U-Boat on the prowl along his route.

Kapitänleutnant Otto Steinbrinck had joined the Kaiserliche Marine on 3rd March 1907. By 1916, he had served on three U-Boats: the U6, UB10 and UB18. In November 1916, he commanded the UC65 which was a smaller Type UCII coastal mine laying submarine. It had distinctive vertical tubes along the centreline. The UC65 was about 49 metres long and powered by a 500hp engine. It was armed with an 88mm deck gun, 7 torpedoes and 18 mines. The top speed was 12 knots on the surface and 7 knots submerged. In May 1917, it operated as part of the Flanders Flotilla and made numerous forays into the

Irish Sea to look for soft targets. This was the time of the unrestricted warfare, which had been declared on the 1st February 1917, and consequently all merchant ships were in grave danger from the silent attacks by the silver fish. On that night, the UC65 was hunting near Ballyhalbert Bay and managed to stop and capture a number of merchant ships. He had already sunk two merchant ships, the British steamer DORA at 00.30 hours and later the Japanese steamer TAIZAN MARU carrying iron ore at 04.30 hours. The first ship attacked off Ballyhalbert was SAINT MUNGO a 402-ton coal boat that was stopped by gunfire at 4.45 am. The twelve-man crew were allowed to take to the lifeboats and row ashore after scuttling charges had been placed on board the coaster. The steamer sank at 5.15 am about two miles from the South Rock light vessel.

Next was the SS DERRYMORE, another steamer of 485 tons sailing light from Dublin to Troon. The captain had seen the SAINT MUNGO go down and tried to escape the submarine by sailing into shallow water near Ballyhalbert. The eleven crew were forced to abandon ship after gunfire and made their way ashore as their boat went down. The captain of the DERRYMORE put the time of the attack at 5.25 am and the ship went down at 5.45 am.

The AMBER was a 401-ton coal boat on the Troon - Waterford route and it was part of the John Kelly fleet. The Master was John Bennett and the crew sighted the U-Boat shelling a steamer off Ballyhalbert at 5.30 am. The Master had been zigzagging south at a steady 8 knots. The U-Boat opened up with the deck gun and fired three shells over the steamer in quick succession. The captain put the helm hard a port and steered for land. As a sign of distress, they sounded the steam whistle. Confidential papers were quickly burnt by the Master. Her crew were again forced to abandon ship and send their small boat over to the submarine. The ship was then boarded by an enemy officer who planted two bombs in the forward hold engine room and one over the side amidships. The Master, Chief Engineer and one Fireman had to ferry the German officer to and from the submarine. The ten British crew were allowed to row ashore in their small boats to Ballyhalbert. The ship sank at 6.15 am.

Number four was the MORION, a cargo vessel of 299 tons, sailing from Dublin to Carnlough and she was in ballast. The Master, Gibson Wilkinson, was 4 miles South South East of the Skullmartin Light Vessel when he saw the U-Boat. He also saw a 3 masted schooner bearing about 10 miles off to the North North East and a steamer sinking North West by West about 4 miles away. She was forced to stop by two shells fired from the deck gun of the U-Boat. The Master lamented the poor behaviour of some of his crew who lowered one of the lifeboats after the second shell was fired. Two Engineers, two Firemen and one Seaman got in the lifeboat and left the ship leaving the Master, Mate and one Seaman on board. This lifeboat was ordered alongside the submarine and was used to ferry the bombs to the steamer. The Master managed to throw the confidential papers overboard and watched them sink. One officer from the submarine planted scuttling charges on board which exploded about 6.35 am. The ship went down just after 7.00 am. The 8-man crew all survived by rowing the lifeboats to shore at Ballyhalbert.

The Master described the submarine as 150 feet long with one deck gun visible and painted grey to the fore from the conning tower. The gun and rest of the hull were painted black. The officers had peaked caps with badges and dark blue overcoats while the ratings had plain peaked caps, leather coats and sea boots. The UC65 steered southward on the surface at about 6 knots towards the smoke of another steamer. This steamer turned out to be an oiler under escort by an armed trawler. This vessel engaged the submarine and there was an exchange of three shots from each one.

At 07.40 hours, the UC65 was attacked by a Naval Patrol Vessel towing six lifeboats and quickly submerged. She steered away from the coast and surfaced later on a calm sea with good visibility.

(Note that the timings of the sinkings have been taken from the Official Reports and hence differ from the following notes.) There seems to be only one local record of the encounter with the submarine and that was from John McGeean, Mate of the South Rock Light Vessel Petrel and he reported the following to the Irish Lights Office.

These are his notes: -

'At 3.00 am on the morning of 2nd May 1917 heard 3 shots from east of ship (the light vessel). At 3.30 explosions from east and after saw submarine on top of water going to another S/S. Submarine fired again S/S blown up. Submarine going again blown another S/S and another. Total number sunk by submarine 5 S/S morning of 2-5-1917. Ships boats full of people pulling from South Rock Lightship at 5.00 am and took all on board and towed the 3 small boats after Patrol Boat and going after submarine dived and disappeared. Submarine visible from 3.30 to 5.30 am 2-5-1917.'

All the crew were allowed to take to the small boats in this incident. Like a lot of these encounters, the submarine commander became a maritime legend in local folklore. Otto Steinbrinck is remembered for his black humour and it was said by one local wit that as one small boat pulled away from a sinking vessel he shouted from his conning tower "If you hurry you will be in time to catch O'Brien's bus from Ballywalter for Belfast!"

The fifth boat mentioned in this report was the EARNEST with Captain James Ferguson and crew on board. The sub caught the schooner six miles southeast of the Skullmartin Lightship and she was a sitting duck as there was no wind to generate more than a lazy speed of one knot per hour. Initially Captain Ferguson and his crew saw the U-Boat at 7.30 am and thought it was a sailboat; but as it approached it lowered its sails, a clever ruse de guerre, and the German sailors started to use the deck gun. A warning shot was fired at 8.15 am from a range of 50 yards straight through a canvas sail on the schooner! There was rifle fire as well. The UC65 quickly established that the schooner was not a Q-ship (A schooner fitted with concealed guns used to sink submarines.

Examples were the RESULT and HELGOLAND.) The crew was given five minutes to abandon ship and allowed to take to the small boat. They were directed to the submarine deck and questioned about the cargo. Standard questions about where to, where from all in superior English from the submarine commander who was described as clean shaven, young, good looking with a fresh complexion. The officers were smartly turned out in uniforms, but the rest of the crew were shabbily dressed in civilian clothes. Steinbrink appeared very anxious to get bombs on board the schooner as soon

as possible. The crew was ordered to row a German officer back to the schooner in their small boat. This officer then planted the scuttling charges on board the EARNEST. He got into conversation with James Ferguson and said that his U-Boat was one of the small ones. He boasted that this was the sixth ship they had sunk that day and must have had a sense of guilt about robbing a schooner man of his ship and his livelihood. Later back at the submarine, the commander apologised to Captain Ferguson for sinking his vessel and in a bizarre form of recompense, he gave him his binoculars! These binoculars stayed with the captain and later became a source of fascination for the young Alan Crozier in 'Harbour House' guesthouse on the Harbour Road. The schooner must have sunk sometime after 8.30 am and the four-man crew were picked up by the patrol vessel, H.M.T. GOSHAWK II at 10.35 hours and landed at Larne harbour.

H.M.T. GOSHAWK II saw the U-Boat about 8.00 am alongside the EARNEST bearing about Southeast by South 4 to 5 miles from Skullmartin Light Vessel. She steamed at full speed towards the U-Boat for 15 minutes and saw the schooner sinking by the head. Five minutes later the captain considered himself to be within range and opened fired on the enemy submarine. The submarine appeared to stop and canted with his broadside to the trawler. GOSHAWK fired two more rounds and the next one, was a misfire. While drawing the faulty cartridge and preparing another, the submarine listed to starboard and disappeared. They steamed over the spot of the crash dive and cruised around for half an hour but saw no sign of oil or anything on the surface of the calm sea. James Ferguson confirmed that the U-Boat went south and dived with a big list. He estimated the U-Boat to be 150 feet long with a beam of 16 feet. He noted the periscope and one gun, about a three pounder, abaft the conning tower. He commented on the new paint, which was light grey forward and dark grey aft. I found James Ferguson's sketch of the U-Boat in the archives and I have reproduced it here with his notes. I was disappointed with this effort because his schooner paintings show such a good eye for detail and artistic ability.

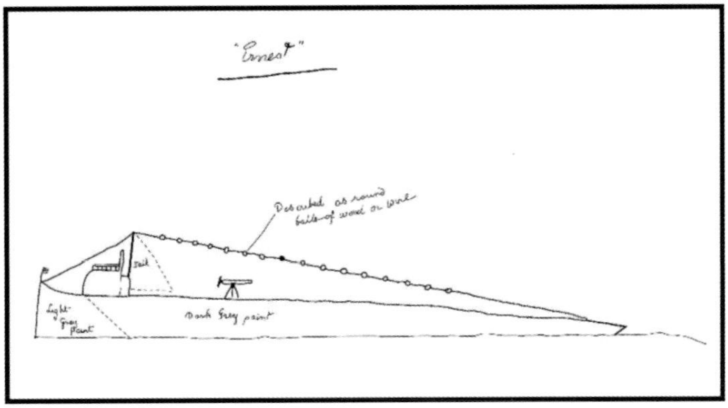

Otto Steinbrinck's War Diary for 2nd May1917 records the incident as follows: -

'08.50 Surfaced and steered away from the coast.
10.00 hours. English three-mast schooner 'Earnest' from Preston (111 tons) to Dublin with coal cargo stopped and sunk with high explosive shells. Meanwhile the alarm seems to be raised; fish trawlers show up from everywhere; one of them turns directly towards the U-Boat and opens fire. Due to the smooth sea and the long distance visibility it seems to me wiser to disappear. I intend to put the U-Boat on ground at the Ardglass Bight and since there is nothing to be achieved by torpedo throughout daylight hours due to the sea state, I will attempt to seek conditions for torpedo attack during moonlight.

10.30 Dived and steered at 30 metres. Around noon 4 depth charges drop; there is however no vessel in sight, which might mean they were air dropped. During afternoon several fish trawlers with white painted radio masts, yachts, motor boats and a destroyer show up and search the area guided by a small airship.'

Steinbrink's timing for the sinking of the EARNEST is wrong and it must have taken place around 8.30 am G.M.T. when cross-referenced with the James Ferguson report and GOSHAWK report made at Larne on the day.

The UC65 proceeded south along the Irish coast and on the 4th May continued to sink fishing vessels and cargo ships. Tragically in one of these incidents near Tuskar Rock, the sinking of the Liverpool cargo ship PILAR DE LARRINAGA, led to 20 merchant seamen being lost.

Although this was the time of the unrestricted attacks on Allied and neutral shipping around Great Britain and Ireland where vessels could be attacked without warning, it was still common for acts of humanity to be exercised by the U-Boat captains. There are other records of safe conduct during the sea war. On the 25th September 1916, the notorious U57 nearly wiped out the Scarborough trawling fleet in a single night. The U-Boat commander there said: "Sorry I have to sink you but it is war. This is the twenty first today." The U57 destroyed 29 trawlers in three days. Closer to home, the Kilkeel fishing fleet was attacked by UB64 under Kaptlt Von Schrader, 12 miles off the Mourne coast on the 30th May 1918. This incident will be covered in detail in a later chapter.

A James Ferguson
Schooner
Name Unknown

In some incidents involving steamers in the Irish Sea the U-Boat crews often offered cigars and cigarettes to the merchant seamen when on board the submarine. There was evidence of such offers in the sinking of the LINDA BLANCHE and KILCOAN in particular. However, I have not heard any mention of a British captain receiving a pair of binoculars. Maybe this was not a gift for James Ferguson but a piece of advice to use binoculars next time so that he would not confuse a fishing boat with a disguised submarine! This is all speculation on my part but, unfortunately, James Ferguson and James M^c^Kee lost a rare 3 masted schooner, which had not even seen a year of service. It is a real pity that no photographs exist of this vessel.

In all of these incidents and similar off the North of Scotland there is no record of anybody receiving a souvenir from the submarine commander. In fact, it was common for the U-Boat crew to take trophies from the merchant ships as proof of a kill. Captain James Ferguson was the exception to this rule. He received a souvenir from the submarine commander!

Not all German U-Boat commanders in World War One were sympathetic to merchant sailors and trawler fishermen. A lot were sunk without warning because fishing boats and schooners were often pressed into service laying anti-submarine nets, tracking U-Boats, acting as decoys and sweeping mines. There are many records of fishing boat sinkings and deaths around the Irish coastline. Germany and Britain both operated blockades of ports and both countries tried to deprive the civilian population of food supplies and coal in particular. In 1917, the German population was starving and thousands died from lack of food and hypothermia. In such circumstances, the unrestricted submarine warfare was born.

Submarine UC65

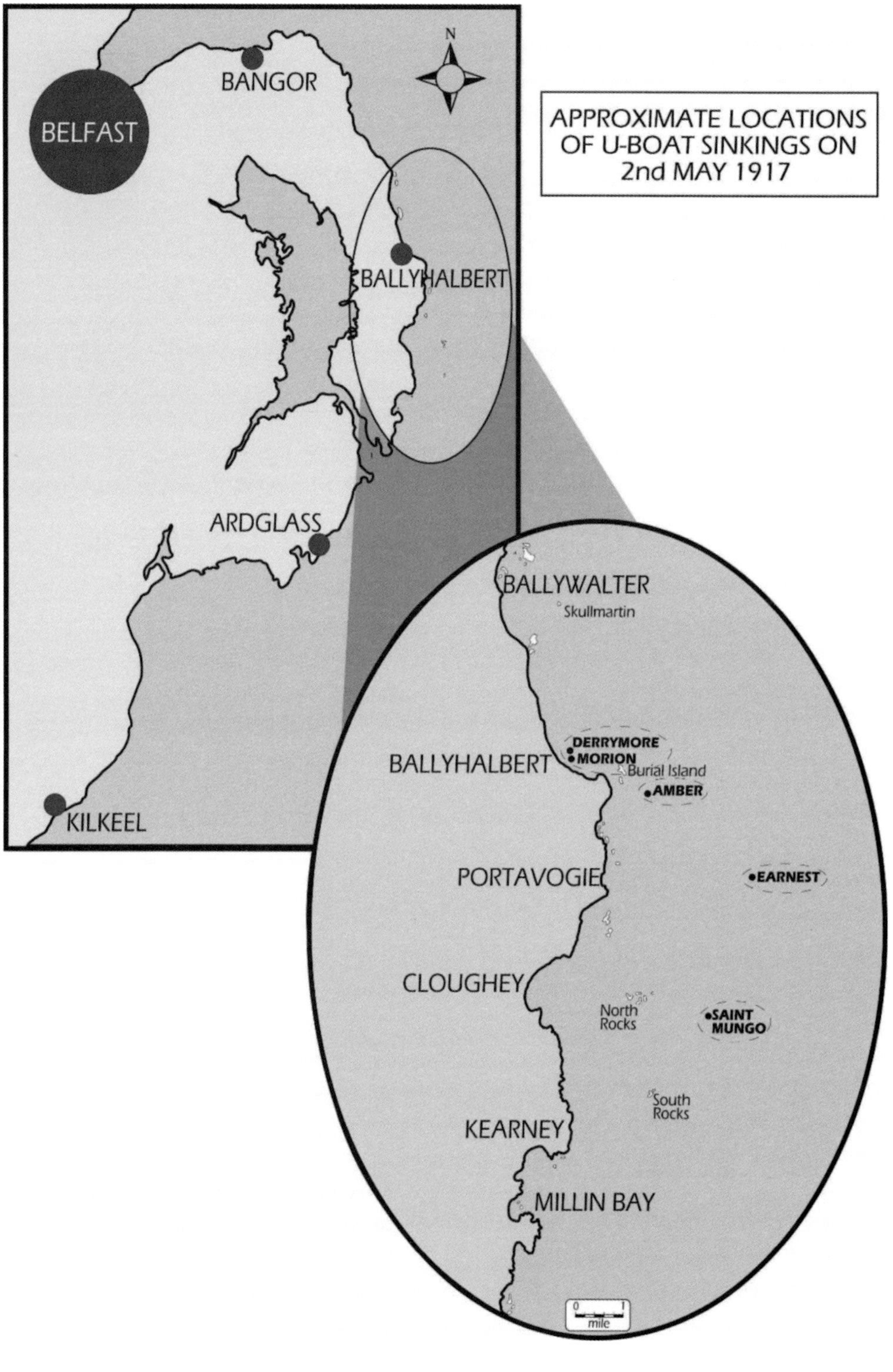
APPROXIMATE LOCATIONS OF U-BOAT SINKINGS ON 2nd MAY 1917
BELFAST
BANGOR
N
BALLYHALBERT
ARDGLASS
KILKEEL
BALLYWALTER
Skullmartin
DERRYMORE
MORION
BALLYHALBERT
Burial Island
AMBER
EARNEST
PORTAVOGIE
CLOUGHEY
North Rocks
SAINT MUNGO
South Rocks
KEARNEY
MILLIN BAY
0
1
mile

OTTO STEINBRINCK

The UC65, which was launched on 8th July 1916, was credited with sinking 105 ships by torpedo, deck gun or mines laid. The H.M. Sub C15, with Lt. E.H. Dolphin in charge, finally sank it on 3rd November 1917 off Beachy Head at 50N 0027E. Twenty-Two German sailors died in this encounter and there were only five survivors. Kaptlt Otto Steinbrinck was not on board the UC65. He had already transferred to the UB57. Divers who have explored the wreck of the UC65 report that it is in two sections with the deck gun still in place.

Kaptlt Otto Steinbrinck

Kaptlt Otto Steinbrinck was born in Lippstadt, Westphalia on 19th December 1888 and joined the navy in 1907. He was a well-decorated officer and deemed a submarine ace in 1915 after sinking 27 merchant ships. He was awarded the Blue Max and the Iron Cross First Class for his efforts.

In 1916, when on board the UB18 he sank even more merchant ships (64) and one submarine, the E22. It is this latter incident which is worthy of note and gained respect for Otto Steinbrinck from friend and foe. On 25th April 1916, Steinbrinck sunk the British submarine E22 off Yarmouth. There were only two survivors on the surface from the E22 and Steinbrinck brought his U-Boat, the

villagers were still talking about his two rescues to sailors from Kilkeel who had stopped off on their way across the Irish Sea.

The HENRIETTA crew in 1930 was made up of James Ferguson, Master, age 57, Hugh Ferguson, Mate, age 54, William McKee age 24 and Joseph Morgan age 40. In the latter half of the year, there was only a three-man crew made up of James and Hugh Ferguson and Joseph Morgan. They rehearsed their lifeboat drill and inspected lifesaving equipment every week. A good policy as this ketch had to negotiate more than its fair share of bad weather while crossing the Irish Sea.

Voyages on the HENRIETTA varied in length from one day for Kilkeel to Liverpool on the 7th August 1930 to ten days on the way back on the 16th August. The ship completed another run from Birkenhead to Kilkeel in under three days on the 1st July 1930. The ketch was based at Kilkeel and mostly sailed to Liverpool, Birkenhead or Douglas on the Isle of Man.

The HENRIETTA ketch acquired an educational role in the 1930's when she was sold to Gordonstoun School in Scotland. My uncle, Charlie Maginnis and Big Tom Newell sailed the HENRIETTA from Kilkeel through the Caledonian Canal to the school that was set up by Kurt Hahn on the east coast of Scotland near Elgin. The boat was fitted out with twenty cabins and it was used to teach the boys to sail. The Kilkeel men showed the boys the ropes and sails and helped them on their expedition from Hopeman to the Norwegian Fiords on board the ketch in 1936. A student on the converted ketch was none other than the young Prince Philip, who gained his love for the sea from such expeditions and the helpful efforts of two Kilkeel schooner men associated with James Ferguson.

In 1927, Captain James Ferguson owned a 53 foot by 15-foot fishing boat of 26 tons called the GOLDEN STREAM. It was built in 1879 at Peel in the Isle of Man and it was rigged as a Nobby with a lug, foresail and mizzen sail. She carried a six-man crew and one boy. James Ferguson acted as skipper along with Thomas Edgar. By 1932, both men had a stake in the boat and Thomas Edgar acted as skipper. On the 18th February 1935, this boat was destroyed by fire in an unfortunate accident in Kilkeel Harbour. There were insurance issues involved in this accident and it was yet a further addition to his toll of losses.

Ketch HENRIETTA at Hopeman
(*Photo courtesy Gordonstoun School*)

RETIREMENT

In retirement, the Captain continued to live on the Harbour Road close to the harbour, which was the focal point of his life. He often walked down the lane near his home to meet up with the ageing schooner crews of a bygone day. The power of the wind had been replaced by powerful Kelvin engines and the wooden hulls by steel. In later life, he walked with a stick. He probably took his prized binoculars with him to scan the horizon for that rare sight of a sailing ship in the distance. His daughter's guesthouse business was continuing to expand at what is now the 'Seaview' site and he had a steady supply of new guests to tell stories of his many voyages and shipwrecks. He was a dedicated family man until the end.

Howard Forsythe of Kilkeel recounted an interesting anecdote about Jimmy Ferguson during the war years. He told me that the Captain often listened to Lord Haw Haw on the radio during the Second World War and the propaganda being broadcast often sent him into a rage, so much so that the radio was in danger of being wrecked! Perhaps he was reminded of the painful loss of the EARNEST in 1917.

He passed away in Downpatrick Infirmary on the 4th April 1945 and his funeral took place on Friday 6th April 1945 from his Harbour Road residence to Mourne Presbyterian Church. Members of the Rural and Urban Councils and crews from the harbour fleet were in attendance. Captain James Ferguson had been in failing health for about five months. The chief mourners at the funeral were: Mrs Mary Ferguson (wife), Robert James Ferguson (son), Margaret, Isabella and Marian (daughters), W. Cromie, S. Crozier (sons-in–law), Hugh and John Ferguson (brothers), Chief Petty Officer Joseph, Hugh, Frank and James Henry (nephews). He was buried in the Old-New burial ground near the old Provincial Bank garden wall in Kilkeel. Perhaps he should have been buried at sea, as it had such an influence on his life and also because it tried to claim him many times on his storm-tossed voyages.

Captain James Ferguson

The binoculars belonging to Otto Steinbrinck, which marked the chance encounter between two men of the sea in the midst of the Great War, have still not been found. Their whereabouts remain a mystery! They were the catalyst for this story of a schooner man and his sailing ships. They have helped keep the memory of James Ferguson alive and that is a reward in itself.

SOURCES OF INFORMATION

I am grateful for the help given to me by the following people, friends, organisations and written sources.

1 Alan and Wilma Crozier of Warrenpoint

2 Ian Taylor, Canterbury

3 Dr Royan Norton, Belfast

4 Vince Jones of Moelfre Lifeboat Station, Anglesey

5 Cecil Trimble, Kilkeel

6 Louise Avery, archivist Gordonstoun School.
For the 'Henrietta' Voyage of 1936 and permission to use the photograph of the ketch at Hopeman

7 Amos Ferguson, Kilkeel (James Ferguson's Paintings)

8 Jim Blaney, Lurgan.
First World War 'The Great War and the Upper Ards' Journal of the Upper Ards Historical Society - No. 6 1982

9 Captain James Moore, Portavogie

10 Staff at the Carnegie Library Bangor, also Newtownards, Donaghadee, Downpatrick & Portaferry Libraries

11 Michael McCaughan, Ulster Folk and Transport Museum, Cultra

12 Bill Quinn, Boat builder, Kilkeel

13 Horst Bredow and Peter Monte, German U-boat Museum and Archive, Cuxhaven. I am especially grateful to Peter Monte for his translation of the war diary of the UC65

14 Lily McKee, Kilkeel

15 Howard Forsythe, Kilkeel

16 Conor Keenan, Nautilus Centre, Kilkeel. Families at Sea Project 2010

17 u.boat.net. World War I

18 Frank and John Maginnis, Kilkeel

19 National Archives at Kew. ADM 137/2962; BT99/3290; BT99/4038

20 'Shipwreck Index of Ireland' by Richard and Bridget Larn 2002 published by Lloyd's Register - Fairplay Ltd

21 J. Ross, The Editor of the Outlook Newspaper 2011

22 Public Record Office NI. TRANS/2A/53/56/A+B; TRANS 2A/47/23A+B

23 CLIP – CREW LIST INDEX PROJECT
an excellent web-site giving BT99 & BT110 references held at the National Archives

APPENDIX

THE LADY LILFORD TRAGEDY 1911

This event took place more than 100 years ago when the Titanic was being built in Harland and Wolff. I decided to write it up in some detail because the schooner was part owned by James Ferguson and James McKee and also because I have never read anything about this tragic collision in the standard reference books.

The Lady Lilford was one of the smaller schooners in the McKee /Ferguson partnership. She was a two-master about 73 feet long and 17 feet wide. She came from the Whitehaven shipyard of Hugh Williamson in 1862 and was registered in Greenock. In 1908, she sailed with an experienced crew led by James Ferguson as Master, James Maginnis as Mate, Joseph Ferguson and Thomas McKee as ABs (Able Seamen). James Maginnis became the Master in July 1908 and he was assisted by Charles Maginnis as Mate and Frank Teggarty as AB (Able Seaman). Voyages were made from Kilkeel to Cardiff, Carnarvon, Dundalk, Pembroke, Rostrevor, Liverpool and Annalong.

On the 24th July 1911, this Kilkeel owned schooner was in Glasgow on the Clyde, laden with a cargo of firebricks. She left Prince's Dock and was towed out by the tug Dauntless to wait for the next tide off Greenock. She was equipped with one small boat, lifebuoys and lifebelts. The vessel was bound for Port Talbot and manned by a four-man crew. Her progress south was hindered by unfavourable southeast winds.

The SS Antrim was a Midland Railway Steamer 330-foot-long and over 2,000 gross tons. She was employed on the Belfast to Heysham route and on the night of 26th July 1911 she left Belfast at 10.42 pm with a crew of 45 and 106 passengers on board. She set sail on the flood tide down the lough and by 11.50 pm she was abeam of Mew Island about one mile away. She was steaming at full speed ahead at 20 knots propelled by her 357 hp (horse-power) engine.

The course was altered from east by quarter south to east-southeast. On the deck of the ANTRIM were the Master John Jackson, Second Officer John Mayor and five hands. A lookout was up on the bridge. Shortly after 11.50 pm, a small schooner showing a green light was sighted close ahead, probably 200 yards from the ANTRIM. The ANTRIM stopped her engines and reversed but it was too late and the sheer power, weight and speed of the steamer ran the schooner down and she sank immediately. Captain Jackson said he heard a voice in the water shouting for help and it took about 8 minutes to launch the lifeboat. A search was carried out for an hour and no wreckage or body was found. The ANTRIM proceeded on her crossing to Heysham and reported the collision to the harbour authorities at 7 am.

James McKee as Managing Owner of the vessel would have assumed on July 27th that the schooner was still en route to Port Talbot. This voyage against a SE wind could take up to a week. Therefore, the Kilkeel owners had no idea that the victim of the collision was the LADY LILFORD. The Belfast Harbour Master, Captain John McIntyre, dispatched the steam tender HELEN MAY to the lough pilots to try and ascertain the name of the schooner. This was now July 28th and it was a time of great anxiety on both sides of the channel. It was thought that no Kilkeel vessel was missing and in fact, on July 29th, it was reported in the press that the MARY ROSANNA from Dublin was the schooner that had been run down. This vessel, on a voyage from Swansea to Campbeltown with a cargo of coal had been due to pass the Copeland Islands at the time of the collision.

It was not until August 9th that Lloyd's Kilkeel agent telegraphed that James McKee reported that the LADY LILFORD was missing and had not been seen since she left Glasgow on 24th July. This news must have been shocking for the families of the crewmembers. James Ferguson was not on board this ship but two of the crew were from the Harbour Road. By August 10th an attempt was made to name the sailors and expressions of sympathy were extended to their families. The crew was made up of a Captain, Mate and two seamen. William McKee was named as the Captain, aged 29 and unmarried. He was the son of another James McKee on the Harbour Road, Kilkeel. Thomas McKee acted as Mate and he was 27 years old with a wife and two children. He was the son of Mr Robert McKee and nephew of the owner of the vessel. He was Howard Forsythe's uncle. The other ABs on board were Cecil Benest, 21 years old from St. Sampson in the Channel Islands, who tragically lost a brother in Kilkeel Bay two years before this collision, and the fourth man was a young lad from Dublin called James Smyth, aged 19.

The Board of Trade Inquiry into the 'Collision off the Copelands' took place in late October 1911 in Liverpool. This was a one-sided affair because none of the schooner's crew survived and most of the evidence came from the Captain and crew of the SS ANTRIM. However, certain questions were raised about the ANTRIM's version of events.

Second Officer Mayor was recalled and questioned about an alteration he had made in a scrap logbook and bridge course-book which he kept at the time the Mew Island light was abeam from 11.51 pm. The suggestion being made that the alterations in the various times of the course had been changed to account for the time at which the collision was stated to have taken place. The Second Officer strenuously denied he had made any alterations or that there had been any collusion between himself and Captain Jackson with reference to alterations.

The book was handed round the Court for inspection and all the members agreed that an alteration had been made. The witness again said there was no alteration in the figure, the seeming alteration being caused by a little bit of dirt on the pen. The court however, adhered to their opinion.

The Chief Engineer, Percy Hughes told of orders being given to stop and reverse the engines, these were promptly carried out in less than two minutes.

Seaman Archibald Brown at the wheel said he heard the lookout report something and the Master gave orders to hard starboard the helm. Brown said the collision occurred 10 seconds from receiving this order and before the course could be altered.

Arthur Sloan, seaman, one of the lookout men and first to report the schooner's light said that it was only 200 yards away before the collision. At first, he thought it was a haze of smoke as the light was so bad and indistinct. Initially he had been on the forecastle to keep a lookout but had to move to the bridge because the spray was coming over the bows.

James McKee, Managing Owner of the LADY LILFORD said that the schooner was well found in every respect. The schooner had been examined by a Board of Trade Surveyor on 9th June 1911 and rated above average for this class of vessel.

Mr Birkett, acting for James McKee, said that he would assume that the schooner hit by the ANTRIM was the LADY LILFORD. He submitted that the collision ought never to have happened and there was no excuse for it. It was a clear night and the schooner's sails should have been seen. There was evidence that a sail had been seen and sailing ships had the right of way. The lookout saw a green light but the excuse put forward was that this light was **dim**! He said that the Court would have to consider whether a proper lookout was kept on the ANTRIM and whether the light was a dim one.

Mr Birkett criticised the evidence of the lookouts, Sloan and Dumigan. In his opinion, Sloan should never have been a lookout. He had no experience as a sailor, only having served on a river steamer at New York for 11 months. Everything pointed to a light been spotted just as the ANTRIM was changing course.

Birkett questioned the starboarding manoeuvre given that the schooner was right under the port bow. Should he not have ported the helm and stopped his engines?

John McDonald, Constable at Port Ellen, Islay produced wreckage (stern boards) from the 2nd and 3rd August with the name LADY LILFORD. He also found a box containing letters addressed to 'C. Benest schooner LADY LILFORD' on the 4th August near Port Ellen. Finally, on the 9th August, a badly decomposed body was washed up at Laggan Bay, Islay but it could not be identified.

Eventually the judgment of the Board of Trade Inquiry was given on Monday 23rd October 1911 at Liverpool. The findings were that the SS ANTRIM was not at fault.

The Court was satisfied from the evidence that the vessel with which the ANTRIM collided was the schooner LADY LILFORD owned by the Kilkeel men.

The collision took place at 11.53 pm on 26th July off Mew Island.

The vessels were very close when evasive action took place.

The steamer and schooner did carry the lights required for night-time navigation. A good and proper lookout was kept on board the ANTRIM.

It was the Court's opinion that the collision was due to the dimness of the green light preventing it from being seen in time. The ANTRIM was navigated with proper and reasonable care by an experienced captain. The Master of the ANTRIM was not at fault and the crew did try to render assistance when the collision happened by launching a lifeboat and carrying out a search. The Court saw no need to deal with the Master's Certificate.

I consider this sea tragedy to be one of the most tragic events in the maritime history of Kilkeel. It must have been difficult for all the bereaved to reach some degree of closure given the nature of the incident. The Collision at the Copelands has been neglected in local history books and I hope this short outline will encourage people to delve further into their family and maritime history.

CAPTAIN JOHN McBRIDE
FROM SAIL TO STEAM

A STORMY 1915

1915 was to become the most eventful year for John and the GLENRAVEL. It all started at 4 am on Wednesday morning the 17th February 1915. The GLENRAVEL was caught in a fierce storm and driven ashore onto the rocks of the Fife coast near Crail. The ship was badly holed in the bow and stern by the razor-sharp rocks. She was held fast by the rocky teeth and the only chance of making her seaworthy again would have to wait until the Spring Tides of March and a dollop of good fortune.

The GLENRAVEL first encountered a strong gale near the Firth of Tay as she headed south for Leith laden with a cargo of cement and iron in support of the war effort. Rain, high winds and heavy seas buffeted the steamer and she was forced onto the rocks near Saushope Links about a mile east of Crail Harbour. Signals of distress were sent out and the Crail Rocket Brigade, under the command of the local Coastguard, responded in the darkness and managed to fix a rope from the shore to the ship. A Breeches Buoy was rigged and one member of the crew was eventually landed on shore after a hair-raising journey. Fortunately for John and the rest of the crew the tide was ebbing and they managed to scramble ashore to safety.

After a head count by the Master, it was discovered that one member of the crew was missing - Hugh Moses Donoghue (alias Mosey Donoghue) from Newry Street, Kilkeel. John was sent to look for the tough fireman on the GLENRAVEL which was still being battered by the storm. He made his way forward to the galley and there he found the unconcerned Mosey boiling eggs in a kettle over a fire. He was determined to have his feast and he scooped out his bounty, hardboiled like him, and ate them when he eventually scrambled ashore!

An inspection of the ship showed damage to the keel and rudder. The cargo was salvaged when the storm subsided but the vessel was not re-floated until St. Patrick's Day 1915. This meant that John transferred to the SS GLENDUN, a sister ship owned by the same company. As we shall see, this turned out to be a lucky move for him.

After the storm incident, Mosey Donoghue returned to Kilkeel in early March 1915. He must have been celebrating his good fortune in escaping the storm-ravaged GLENRAVEL because he was charged with having maliciously broken a plate glass window in Jordan's Pub on Newry Street.

JOURNEY'S END FOR THE GLENRAVEL

After repairs, it was back to business for the SS GLENRAVEL with Master Alexander Cameron still in charge and H. T. Owens from Holyhead as John's replacement as 1st Mate. On the 6th of August 1915, the SS GLENRAVEL left Belfast for Leith with 800 tons of cargo (Iron Ore and General Goods) and a complete absence of Mourne Men on the crew list. The ship was manned by

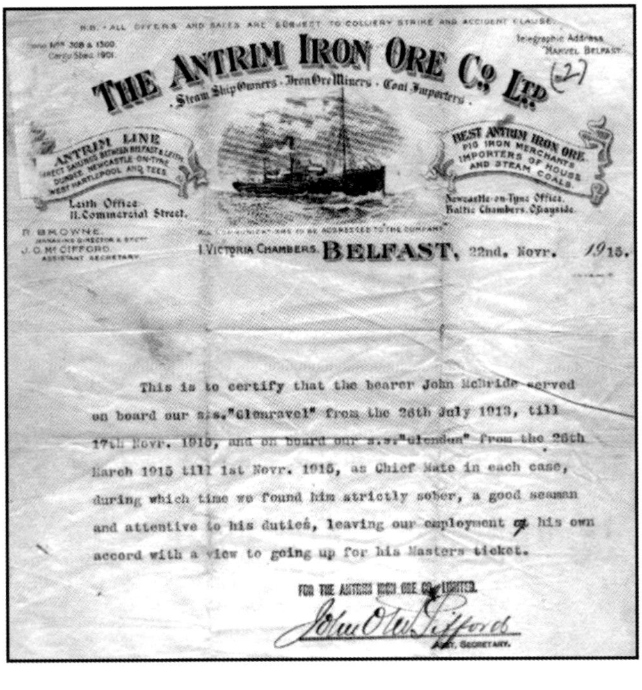

N.B. - ALL OFFERS AND SALES ARE SUBJECT TO COLLIERY STRIKE AND ACCIDENT CLAUSE.

THE ANTRIM IRON ORE Co LTD (2)

Steam Ship Owners · Iron Ore Miners · Coal Importers.

ANTRIM LINE

BEST ANTRIM IRON ORE. PIG IRON MERCHANTS IMPORTERS OF HOUSE AND STEAM COALS.

Leith Office 11, Commercial Street.

Newcastle-on-Tyne Office. Baltic Chambers, Quayside.

R. BROWNE

J. O. McGIFFORD ASSISTANT SECRETARY.

1 VICTORIA CHAMBERS. BELFAST, 22nd. Novr. 1915.

This is to certify that the bearer John McBride served on board our s.s."Glenravel" from the 26th July 1913, till 17th Novr. 1915, and on board our s.s."Glendun" from the 26th March 1915 till 1st Novr. 1915, as Chief Mate in each case, during which time we found him strictly sober, a good seaman and attentive to his duties, leaving our employment of his own accord with a view to going up for his Masters ticket.

FOR THE ANTRIM IRON ORE Co LIMITED.

John O. McGifford

ASST. SECRETARY.

14 crew and they sailed round the north of Scotland and south towards Edinburgh. Around 6.50 am on the 8th of August, a shot was heard and a U-Boat was spotted approaching the vessel from the N.N.E. about 2 miles away. The Master altered his course to head for the nearest land at full speed, a maximum of 10 knots. The U17, commanded by Kplt. Hans Walther, had a superior speed of 15 knots on the surface and began to overhaul the slower steamer. Several more shots

were fired from the deck gun and they landed close to the steamer. After an hour, the chase was nearly over and the U-Boat was about a quarter of a mile away. A British White Ensign was flying on the U17, by now a common ruse. Master Cameron knew he was trapped and he stopped engines and abandoned ship with his crew. Hans Walther steered the U-Boat alongside the GLENRAVEL and placed scuttling charges on board. Explosions were heard after 8.00 am and smoke signalled the death throes of the little steamer. It sank slowly by the stern and, by 10.25 am, it slipped under the water about 25 miles north of Kinnaird Head near Fraserburgh.
All the crew were saved and none were injured. They rowed steadily towards land and were taken in tow by the Fraserburgh Lifeboat, LADY ROTHES, which delivered them safely to shore. There were no confidential papers seized by the enemy but secret navigation instructions were discovered in the Master's bag, later in 1916!

ON THE WHEATFLOWER

Spillers Ltd was a British Company that owned flour-milling operations and bakeries. The Company was established as a flour-milling business by Joel

Spiller in 1829 at Bridgwater. From there, it expanded to Bristol and Cardiff. Joel Spiller and his partner, Samuel Browne, developed steam powered mills and, by 1855, they began to manufacture

ship and dog biscuits. A bakery was purchased in Cardiff to produce these products. By 1889, the Company became a Limited Company under the name of Spiller & Co. (Cardiff) Ltd and, in the same year, the name was changed again to Spillers and Bakers because the firm joined William Baker and Sons from Bristol.

The business continued to expand to London, Newcastle and Birkenhead. Spillers also purchased steamers during the First World War and these vessels were mainly based in Cardiff. Grain was imported from America and the Ukraine and the steamers were used to distribute it from the grain stores. The mills also needed coal and this became an essential cargo not only for their industry but also for trade purposes.

The steamers always had a name beginning with 'WHEAT' - WHEATEAR (1906) 383 gt; WHEATFIELD (1909) 515 gt; WHEATLANDS (1912) 499 gt; WHEATBERRY (1915) 405 gt and WHEATSHEAF (1915) 500 gt.

Captain John McBride became the Master of a smaller coaster called WHEATFLOWER (188 gt) which was registered in Cardiff in 1916. This was a Sunderland built vessel from 1895 and Spillers bought it from John Short Cole in Newcastle-on-Tyne. This was John's first ship as Master.

In early 1916, it seemed appropriate that John had Mourne Men on board his new steamer. He knew them well and John McKee (35 years old) from Kilkeel was Mate and, like John, had experience of sailing vessels. Chambers McBride (20 years old) from Kilkeel was an AB and a young William McBride (17 years old) from Newry was another. The rest of the crew was made up from a variety of nations, Norway, Russia, Arabia and Denmark. William McBride (51 years old) from Kilkeel joined him as Mate on the 1st July 1917.

A lot of their voyages were around South Wales to Haverfordwest, Cardigan, Tenby, Fishguard, Neath, Swansea and across the Irish Sea to Dublin, Wicklow Waterford and Dundalk. In 1917, there was an unrestricted war being waged by the German U-Boats and Captain John had to listen to naval intelligence and follow the safest route.

THE 1918 ATTACK

By early January 1918, Lloyd George spelt out the War Aims of the British Empire including standing by French democracy to the death, a complete restoration of independence and reparation for Belgium, similar justice for Serbia, Montenegro and Romania as well as independence for Poland. This was a sign that doubts had begun to set in and questions were being asked. What was the point of it all? The men in the trench and stench knew the truth.

Elsewhere in the Bristol Channel, another hospital ship, REWA, was torpedoed by the U55, west of Hartland Point. This led to another propaganda war in the press and it became clear that another war crime had been committed since the hospital ship had not broken the conditions laid down by The Hague Convention.

By January 22nd 1918, Sir Edward Carson had tendered his resignation from the War Cabinet to Lloyd George on the grounds that his role there would compromise his stance on the question of Home Rule and Ulster. He returned to Belfast to visit the shipyards and explain his course of action in places such as the Ulster Reform Club.

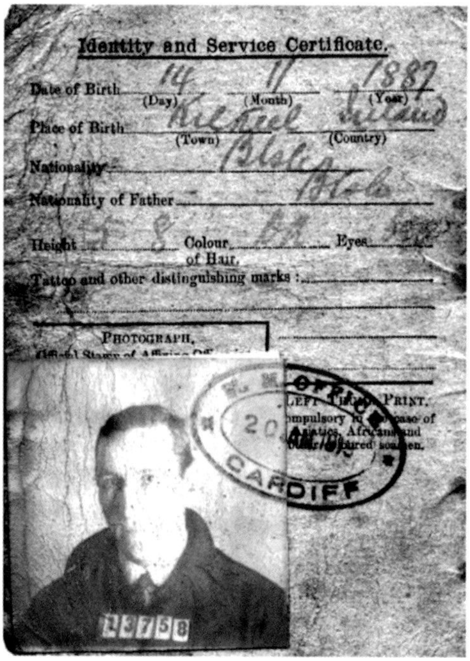

Sir Eric Geddes, First Lord of the Admiralty, declared at the beginning of February 1918 that 'The submarine is held'. He was feeling optimistic after a year of German unrestricted warfare which began on the 1st February 1917. He had grounds for saying this because of the 'curves' (statistics) which showed that the sinking of merchant ships had shown a reduction over the past year.

The Navy had at last adopted the Convoy System and there were better mines, more minefields, depth charges, airships, hydrophone development and Room 40 Intelligence. The latter was Top Secret and the Codebreakers could track individual U-Boats and find their approximate position. Maybe they should have done even better in the earlier stages of the war at sea because British naval Intelligence had all 3 German Codebooks in their possession by November 1914! The Merchant Ship Codebook had been captured in Melbourne in August 1914, the Russians had captured 2 or 3 copies of the main German naval 'signal' book (Signal Buch der Kaiserlichen Marine SKM) and one was delivered to Churchill. The third codebook (Verkehrsbuch) was found under mysterious circumstances in the North Sea on the 30th November 1914. This last one, the *TRANSPORT* book, was used by the U-Boats for transport communication at sea.

However, the UB77 countered Sir Eric Geddes' optimism on the 5th February 1918 by sinking one of the biggest troopships of the war, the Anchor Liner TUSCANIA which was carrying American troops across the Atlantic. Two torpedoes were fired by Kplt. Wilhelm Meyer and the big ship went down 7 miles North of Rathlin Island. There were 166 casualties from this attack despite the fact the ship was in convoy with destroyers in escort.

John McBride had some experience of the convoy system shortly after he joined Spillers. He related an incident, again to Joe Doran, which must have happened in 1917. John was Master of the SS WHEATFLOWER which he had joined on the 2nd February 1916. His voyages now were back and forth across the Irish Sea to places like Cardiff, Bristol, Avonmouth, Neath, Swansea for coal destined for Dublin, Waterford, Cork and Wicklow. On his many voyages, John would encounter many Mourne schooner men and merchant seamen. On one occasion in May 1917 when in convoy from Kingstown (Dunlaoghaire) south to Cork, he met Master John Doran from Kilkeel in command of the GUILD MAYOR schooner on the same convoy south. The schooner depended on a fair wind but, on this occasion the wind failed and the vessel could make no headway. John offered Doran a tow which was gladly accepted. The two ships parted company at Tuskar Rock and, soon after, the GUILD MAYOR became engulfed by thick fog from the east. This resulted in a collision with a Greek freighter lying at anchor. The schooner was badly damaged by the steel hull and foundered the next day, near Tuskar Rock. This navigation reference point was to feature again in another of Captain John M^c^Bride's WHEATFLOWER voyages in early 1918.

LAST VOYAGE OF THE WHEATFLOWER

Captain John left Cardiff on the 17th February 1918 with a cosmopolitan crew on board. The ship was not on Government service and it carried 170 tons of coal for Dublin. John followed the route instructions from Cardiff to Bishops then Tuskar and up inside the banks along the Wicklow coast. He made slow progress because of the route and low power. His speed was only 7.5 knots and he followed instructions on zig-zagging in dangerous waters. He had zig-zagged 2 points either side of the course every 10-15 minutes, to protect the little steamer from a torpedo shot.

By 2.15 pm, on the 19th February 1918, the coaster was 10 miles NW by N from Tuskar Rock. The wind was from the North West (Force 5-6) with a moderate sea and a visibility of 5 miles. Even though there were 3 lookouts on the bridge, the U-Boat was not sighted until after the first shell was fired. The shells were fired from a great distance and the U-Boat had not been spotted because of the low winter sun.

U86

The shells had been fired by the U86 deck gun under the command of Oblt. Helmut Patzig. This U-Boat was a product of a Kiel shipyard and had been built in 1915-16. The deck gun was 105 mm and could be fired accurately from 6,000 yards away. Surface speed could reach 17 knots which was more than twice the speed of the little coaster. Classified as a diesel-powered attack U-Boat with a crew of 35 who maintained the 227-foot silver fish armed with a dozen torpedoes, waiting to be launched via bow and stern tubes.
Helmut Patzig started his attacks in Home Waters on the 14th February 1918 by sinking a soft target, the sailing vessel, BESSIE STEPHENS, carrying a cargo of Cornish china clay. He used the deck gun on the sailing ship before moving on to bigger prey, the SS PINEWOOD (2,219 tons) on the 17th February 1918. This ship had been heading for Queenstown (Cobh) on the Southern Irish coast. The SS WHEATFLOWER was next on his list.
The third shell hulled the coaster and set her on fire. The ship began to sink and John had no choice but to abandon ship. Ten more deck gun shells whistled around the ship before they got away. Fortunately, there were three sailing vessels to the west and one patrol vessel, H.M.T. WHITEFRIARS, astern. When they abandoned the ship, more shells were fired at a rate of one round every 2 minutes. One member of the crew, the Cook, Henry Fahrenkrug, disobeyed John's order to abandon ship and went forward on the WHEATFLOWER to retrieve his kit. Sadly, he was hit by a shell and killed. John estimated that the ship was hit eleven times in total and that 20 rounds were fired after they had abandoned ship.

Their only protection on the coaster was Smoke Apparatus (Pattern A&B) but there had been no time to use it. The 8 survivors got into one lifeboat and the armed trawler sailed in to rescue them by coming between the lifeboat and the U-Boat and firing back. This Hull trawler, H.M.T. WHITEFRIARS (No. 1191) had been hired by the Royal Navy and saw service from 1916 to 1919 as a mine-sweeper. At 135 feet long and 286 gt, armed with a smaller gun (1.12 pounder) which was just big enough to intimidate the U-Boat and drive it underwater. This trawler was en route to Buncrana and further north, the WHEATFLOWER crew was transferred to H.M.D. GOLDEN CHANCE and taken to Larne where John M^c^Bride made his report to the Commodore.

WHEATFLOWER CREW LIST 1918

1	Master John M^c^Bride (30)	Kilkeel Cert. 105868
2	C. Peters (32)	N.B.S. Mate
3	A. Andersen (49)	Norwegian 1st Engineer
4	A. Jamik? (41)	Russian 2nd Engineer
5	*Henry FahrenKrug (54)	N.B.S. Cook (Killed)
6	Geo Alexander (60)	Greek AB
7	William M^c^Bride (51)	Kilkeel AB
8	H. Bohu (39?)	Russian Fireman
9	Ali Mahamad (25?)	Arab Fireman

*Henry Fahrenkrug joined the ship on the 19/6/17 and called himself a 'DANE'. He was from Altona near Hamburg, which had been part of Denmark until the middle of the 19th century. At the time of the attack he was a Naturalised British Subject.

John answered over 50 questions in detail. The coaster had not been boarded by the Germans and no Confidential documents were captured by them. He made a decent attempt to describe the U-Boat. He overestimated its length at 300 feet because he did not see it at close quarters. He noted that the upper deck was rounded off, the oval-shaped conning tower, the life rails all round it and the jump wires from bow to stern over the conning tower. He reported two guns on board the U86, one forward and one abaft the conning tower. The dark grey paint looked new and the conning tower rose straight from the upper deck. The answers were for the Naval Intelligence Department to work out the type of U-Boat and details about wireless gear. He had answered to the best of his ability which was much better than some I have read! More importantly, he did comply with Admiralty and Local Instructions to avoid capture by the enemy. The trawler managed to keep track of the U-Boat as it headed north. Its position was reported to the Navy at Kingstown at 6.30 pm that evening.

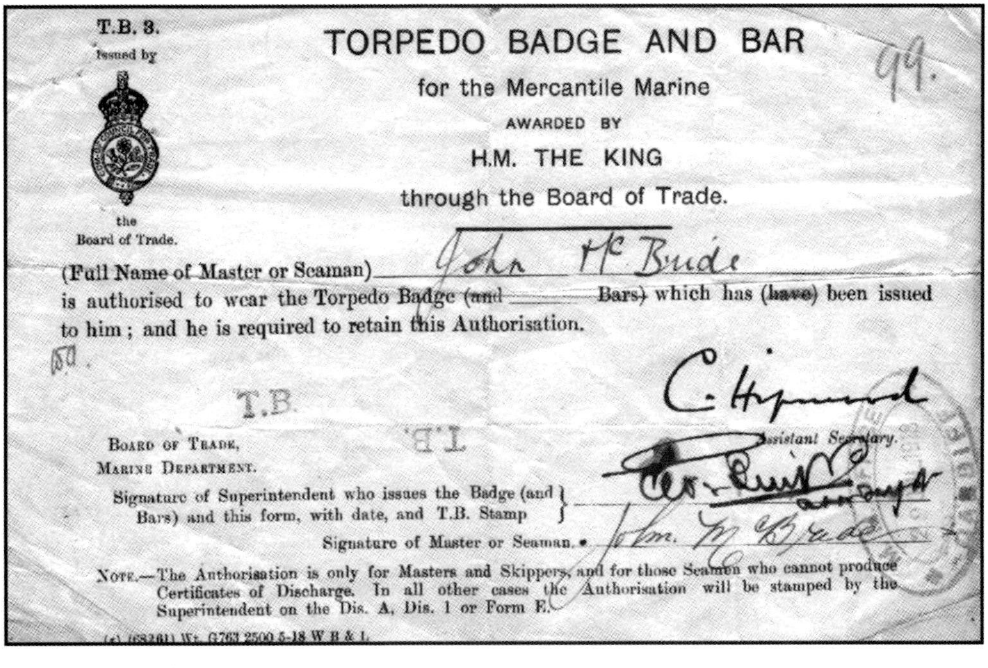

T.B. 3.
Issued by
the
Board of Trade.

TORPEDO BADGE AND BAR
for the Mercantile Marine
AWARDED BY
H.M. THE KING
through the Board of Trade.

99.

(Full Name of Master or Seaman) John McBride
is authorised to wear the Torpedo Badge ~~(and~~ ______ ~~Bars)~~ which has ~~(have)~~ been issued to him; and he is required to retain this Authorisation.

T.B.

C. Hipwood
Assistant Secretary.

BOARD OF TRADE,
MARINE DEPARTMENT.

Signature of Superintendent who issues the Badge (and Bars) and this form, with date, and T.B. Stamp

Signature of Master or Seaman. John McBride

NOTE.—The Authorisation is only for Masters and Skippers, and for those Seamen who cannot produce Certificates of Discharge. In all other cases the Authorisation will be stamped by the Superintendent on the Dis. A, Dis. 1 or Form E.

OBLT. HELMUT PATZIG

John stayed with Spillers after this attack for an extended period of service. Helmut Patzig continued to attack merchant ships, large and small and became a key witness in one of the most controversial incidents near the end of the war. The LLANDOVERY CASTLE was a large liner which had been requisitioned as a HOSPITAL SHIP on charter to the Canadian Government. On the 27th June this ship was returning from Canada with Canadian Army Medical Corps on board, both male and female. They were over 100 miles west of Fastnet when the U86 fired a torpedo into Number 4 Hold at 9.30 pm and the ship began to sink very quickly. The Master, Captain E.A. Sylvester, ordered abandon ship and most of the lifeboats were safely launched. The ship sank in about 10 minutes but the U86 returned to the scene of the crime about 1.5 hours later and began to intimidate and interrogate some of the survivors in an aggressive manner. Lifeboats were scattered in the darkness and the U Boat attempted to ram and skim some of them. The Master's lifeboat had 24 occupants on board and they experienced these manoeuvres. They also witnessed shells being fired into the darkness at unseen targets. The mystery was, 'What were the targets?'

Captain Sylvester headed for the Irish Coast, over 100 miles away and, by a stroke of good fortune, his lifeboat was spotted by a British destroyer on the morning of 29th June 1918. No other lifeboats could be found in the search that followed. There were only 24 survivors out of 234 medical staff and crew. What had happened to the other lifeboats?

It was soon realised that a war crime had been committed by Patzig and some of the crew of the U86. The case of the LLANDOVERY CASTLE was heard at the 2nd Criminal Senate of the Imperial Court of Justice at Leipzig in 1921. Witnesses made up of survivors and U Boat ratings, had gained the impression that the U86, under orders from Patzig, had fired on the lifeboats, killing all survivors including 14 female nurses.

Patzig had also falsified his log book to omit any mention of the hospital ship attack, going so far as to lay a false trail away from the scene of the atrocity. Two lifeboats had disappeared after the shelling. Patzig and three other crew members were found guilty by the Leipzig Court and given a prison sentence. However, Patzig did not even appear in court as he had disappeared in Danzig, his home town, and could not be found. This was all because of a unique status given to Danzig, a technicality on jurisdiction, courtesy of the Versailles Treaty! The whole trial and punishment was a farce and it was strange to find out in my research that Patzig had re-surfaced in World War II and lived until 1984! War is war alright, but war criminals should not escape justice. I think John McBride did the right thing in swiftly abandoning the WHEATFLOWER in 1918, given that he was being shelled relentlessly by the U86.

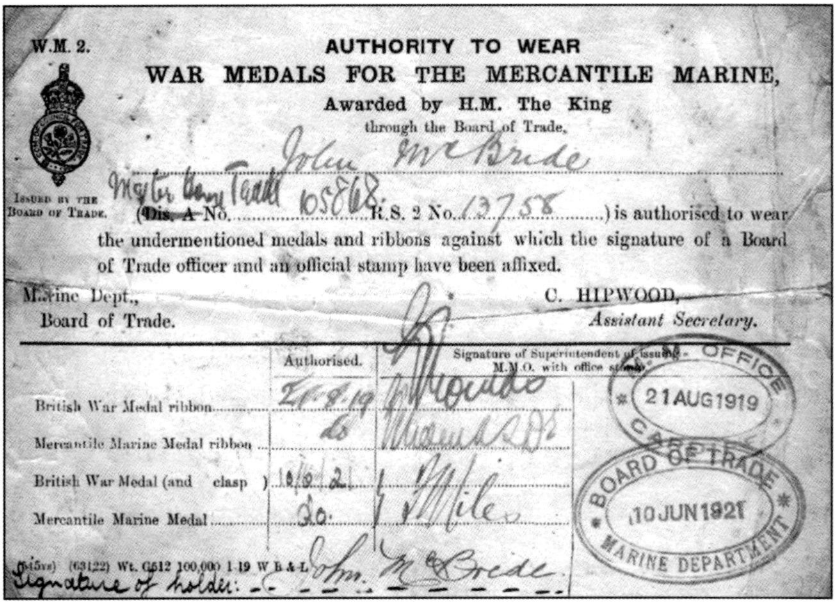
W.M. 2.

AUTHORITY TO WEAR
WAR MEDALS FOR THE MERCANTILE MARINE,
Awarded by H.M. The King
through the Board of Trade,

John McBride

Issued by the Board of Trade.

(Dis. A No. .... R.S. 2 No. ....) is authorised to wear the undermentioned medals and ribbons against which the signature of a Board of Trade officer and an official stamp have been affixed.

Marine Dept.,
Board of Trade.

C. HIPWOOD,
Assistant Secretary.

	Authorised.	Signature of Superintendent of issuing M.M.O. with office stamp.
British War Medal ribbon	21-8-19	
Mercantile Marine Medal ribbon	do	
British War Medal (and clasp)	10/6/21	
Mercantile Marine Medal	do	

21 AUG 1919

BOARD OF TRADE 10 JUN 1921 MARINE DEPARTMENT

Signature of holder: John McBride.

POST WAR WITH SPILLERS

After the end of the war, John stayed. with Spillers and captained steamers with a larger tonnage than WHEATFLOWER. In 1919, he was in charge of the SS WHEATFIELD and towards the end of his Spillers career, SS WHEATHILL. His Cargo Book gives a clear picture of his voyages - date of departure, distance, cargo tonnage, customer and port destination. Flour, bran and wheat were by far the main cargo but there were also seasonal runs to France, Trigeur and Brest from Plymouth. Cargoes in June 1931, included over 2,000 bags of potatoes from Trigeur and 1,564 crates of strawberries from Brest for next day delivery at Plymouth. He was proud of his fast turnaround where soft fruit was involved and won a bonus of £80 in beating the other ships back to Plymouth. In 1930, he sometimes made runs to Kilkeel with 193 tons of coal from Workington and flour for James McKee & Sons. A rare opportunity for him to combine business and family reunion. John parted company with Spillers in January 1933, mainly because his steamer had been sold and there was no other position available. During his time with the Spiller Steamship Branch (1915-1933), the company said that 'Captain McBride has always carried out his duties in a thoroughly competent manner and we have always found him to be of strictly sober habits'. He did not take long to find a new ship to command.

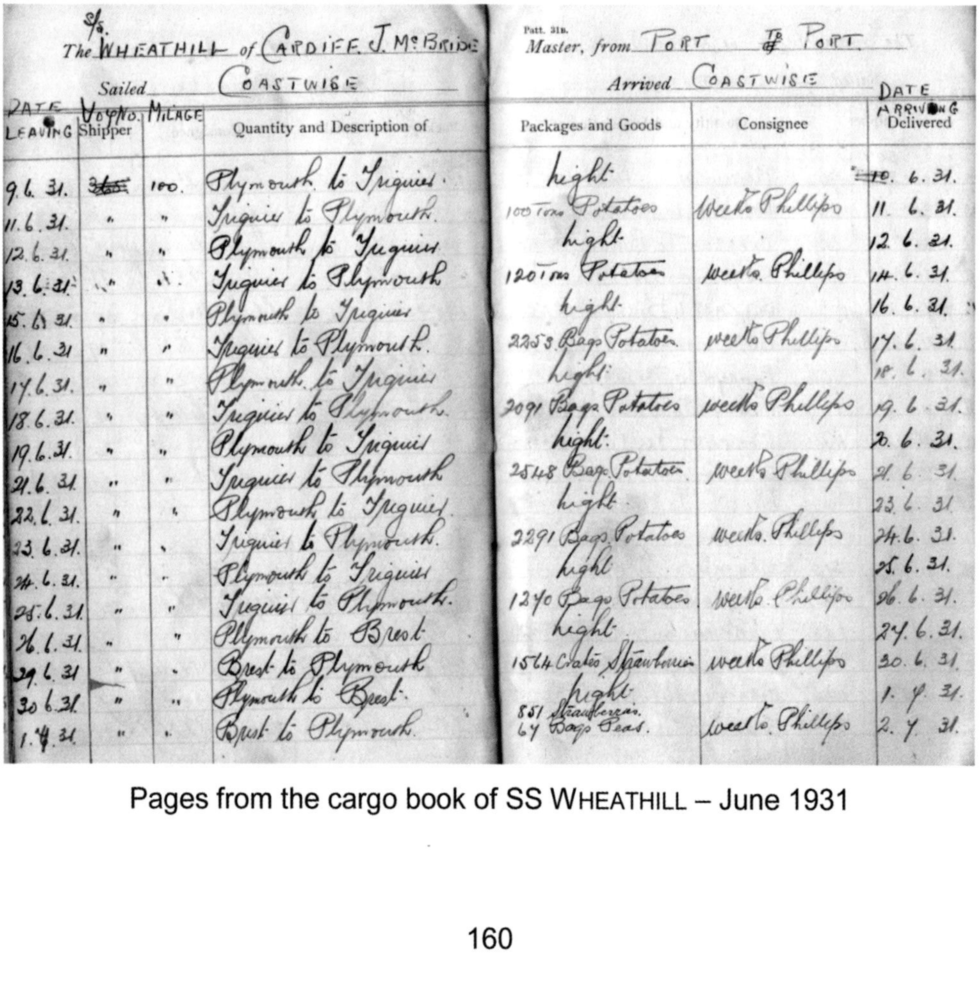
The WHEATHILL of CARDIFF J. McBRIDE Master, from PORT to PORT

Sailed COASTWISE Arrived COASTWISE

DATE LEAVING	VOY No. Shipper	MILAGE	Quantity and Description of	Packages and Goods	Consignee	DATE ARRIVING Delivered
9.6.31	[illegible]	100.	Plymouth to Triguier	Light		10.6.31
11.6.31	"	"	Triguier to Plymouth	100 Tons Potatoes	Weeks Phillips	11.6.31
12.6.31	"	"	Plymouth to Triguier	Light		12.6.31
13.6.31	"	"	Triguier to Plymouth	120 Tons Potatoes	Weeks Phillips	14.6.31
15.6.31	"	"	Plymouth to Triguier	Light		16.6.31
16.6.31	"	"	Triguier to Plymouth	2253 Bags Potatoes	Weeks Phillips	17.6.31
17.6.31	"	"	Plymouth to Triguier	Light		18.6.31
18.6.31	"	"	Triguier to Plymouth	2091 Bags Potatoes	Weeks Phillips	19.6.31
19.6.31	"	"	Plymouth to Triguier	Light		20.6.31
21.6.31	"	"	Triguier to Plymouth	2548 Bags Potatoes	Weeks Phillips	21.6.31
22.6.31	"	"	Plymouth to Triguier	Light		23.6.31
23.6.31	"	"	Triguier to Plymouth	2291 Bags Potatoes	Weeks Phillips	24.6.31
24.6.31	"	"	Plymouth to Triguier	Light		25.6.31
25.6.31	"	"	Triguier to Plymouth	1240 Bags Potatoes	Weeks Phillips	26.6.31
26.6.31	"	"	Plymouth to Brest	Light		27.6.31
29.6.31	"	"	Brest to Plymouth	1564 Crates Strawberries	Weeks Phillips	30.6.31
30.6.31	"	"	Plymouth to Brest	Light		1.7.31
1.7.31	"	"	Brest to Plymouth	851 Strawberries. 67 Bags Peas.	Weeks Phillips	2.7.31

Pages from the cargo book of SS WHEATHILL – June 1931

TOWARDS WORLD WAR II

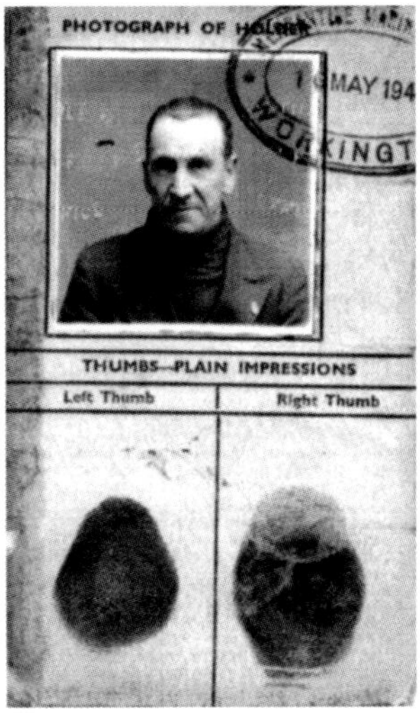

Captain John McBride spent his later years on the Fisher boats from Newry. Although he had spells on the SS BAMBOO and SS OAK, he spent most of his time on the SS PALM. Again, he was conscientious in record keeping for the company and these make interesting reading. There are details of wages to crew members, expenses at ports from Newry to Garston, Insurance Stamps, Telephone Calls, Telegrams, Tide Tables, Lamptrimmer Expenses, Rope Attendance etc. In the 1941 book, I noticed two entries of note which referred to a Gunner on board the SS PALM. There was a weekly Food Allowance for the Gunner of 19s 10d and Wages of 3s 6d (6d per day). I tried to find out more details about this Gunner but, to date, I have not found out his name nor the crew records from World War II.

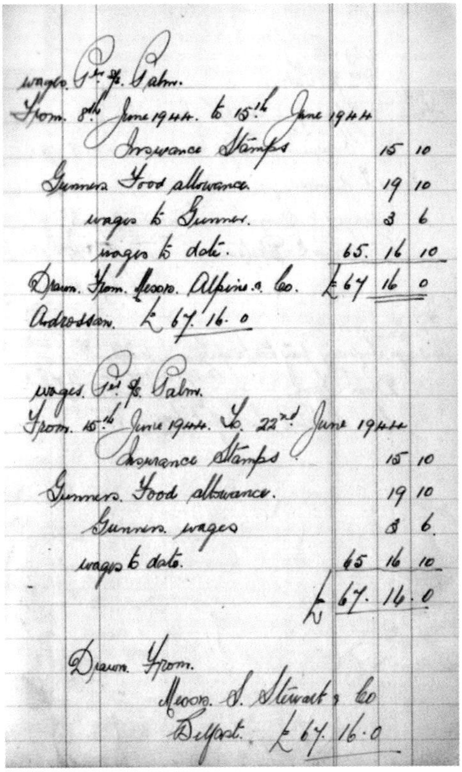
Wages SS Palm.
From 8th June 1944 to 15th June 1944
Insurance Stamps 15 10
Gunners Food allowance 19 10
wages to Gunner 3 6
wages to date 65 16 10
Drawn from Messrs Alpine & Co. £67 16 0
Ardrossan £67.16.0

Wages SS Palm.
From 15th June 1944 to 22nd June 1944
Insurance Stamps 15 10
Gunners Food allowance 19 10
Gunners wages 3 6
wages to date 65 16 10
£67.16.0
Drawn From
Messrs J. Stewart & Co
Belfast £67.16.0

Sean Patterson and James McArevey, both maritime historians from Newry verified that some of the Fisher vessels had Gunners on board during World War II. They were probably trained at the Gunnery School at H.M.S. CAROLINE and provided with Hotchkiss guns for defence against German aerial attacks. The guns were mounted on the bridge and fired 0.303 ammunition. There were no records of any attacks in John McBride's

From left to right---John Shields, Robert Fleming, Captain John McBride, Thomas Fleming and Ned Green plus little Chin Chin who organised the '*Chinwag'* on the 22nd April 1957

SOURCES OF INFORMATION

I am especially grateful for the help given to me by the following people, friends, organisations and written sources.

1 Jean and John Stevenson, Kilkeel

2 Hilary Maginnis, Family Historian

3 Dr Royan Norton, Belfast

4 Sean Patterson, Newry

5 James McArevey, Newry Maritime Association

6 Alan Crozier, Warrenpoint

7 Down Mirror September 1963 (Joe Doran Article)

8 Outlook Newspaper: 5th June 1964, 21st August 1964, 12th February 1965, 18th February 1982

9 Dundee Courier 19th February 1915 (SS Glenravel)

10 Scotsman15 August 1906 (SS Glenravel)

11 News Letter 11th March 1915

12 Census Ireland 1901

13 Public Record Office of Northern Ireland (PRONI)
SS Melissa Crew List 1910 (ON 124672); SS Glenravel Crew Lists 1913 &1914 (ON 120713)

14 National Maritime Museum, Greenwich 1915 Crew Lists

15 The National Archives, Kew. ADM 137/4011 Feb. 15-28, 1918, ADM 137/2959; BT 99/3411 (1918); BT 99/3307 (1917); Home Waters Telegrams ADM 137/693 No.959 19/2/18

16 u-boat.net U86 WW1

17 'Shipwreck Index of Ireland' by R. Larn & B. Larn, Fairplay

18 'Outrage at Sea' by Tony Bridgland (2002), Pen & Sword

Special thanks to Jean and John Stevenson of Kilkeel for giving me permission to study and use a wealth of material on the life of Captain John McBride. Jean is the granddaughter of John McBride and I am so pleased that she had the foresight to value all his photos, log books, cargo books, newspaper articles as 'gold dust' for the family and maritime historian. I have used only a fraction of the material in this chapter and I trust that it does justice to this merchant seaman and how he worked and earned his deserved recognition during the war years.

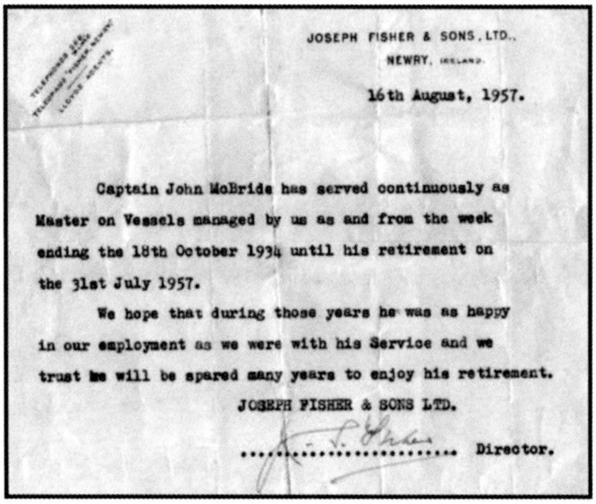

JOSEPH FISHER & SONS, LTD.,
NEWRY, IRELAND.

16th August, 1957.

Captain John McBride has served continuously as Master on Vessels managed by us as and from the week ending the 18th October 1934 until his retirement on the 31st July 1957.

We hope that during those years he was as happy in our employment as we were with his Service and we trust he will be spared many years to enjoy his retirement.

JOSEPH FISHER & SONS LTD.

.... Director.

Farewell from Fishers

ATTACKS ON THE FISHING BOATS 1918

NICKEY

1918

By May 1918, there was much debate about the enforcement of conscription in Ireland. There were occasional lulls in the trenches around Ypres and Baron von Richthofen had already been shot down over the Somme, behind Australian lines. The Royal Navy had carried out daring raids on the ports of Zeebrugge and Ostend in an effort to bottle up the U-Boats. A lot of Ulstermen were involved in these raids which used block ships filled with concrete for sinking in strategic channels. The H.M.S. VINDICTIVE, an obsolete cruiser, was sunk at the entrance to Ostend harbour in a valiant effort to stop the U-Boats.

The U-Boat was now being hunted from the air as well by seaplanes, airships and observation balloons towed along by naval vessels. When spotted they were bombed from the air or depth-charged. However, by the third week in May 1918, the UB64 under the command of Kapitänleutnant Otto von Schrader was already operating in the Irish Sea. He had taken over the UB64 again in February 1918 and, although only 30 years old, he had been decorated with an Iron Cross First Class. On the 23rd May 1918, he was far south of the Mournes and he sunk a passenger steamer, the SS INNISFALLEN, belonging to the City of Cork Steam Packet Company. This took place near the Kish Light Vessel and he was now looking for his next target. The U-Boat headed north.

The sinking of the fishing boats off the Mourne coast in 1918 should not have been a total surprise because there were many incidents of fishing vessels being sunk by U-Boat bombs and shellfire. A year before the Mourne attack, the Baltimore fishing fleet had encountered the UC75 (Oberleutnant Johannes Lohs) a member of the Flanders Flotilla. Seven boats were destroyed off Baltimore, mostly 13 to 14 miles south of the Stags.

The boats lost in this attack were: -

ELEANOR	31 gt*	
FASTNET	31 gt*	
HIBERNIA	21 gt*	
LUCK LASS	10 gt*	
NORTH STAR	15 gt*	
SIR EDWARD BIRKBECK	23 gt*	
CARBERRY KING	31 gt*	fishing fleet drifter

* gt = gross tons

There were no casualties in this incident but what is really interesting is the way it was reported about a month later.

The boats had been fishing for mackerel off Baltimore when they were stopped by the UC75 and the crews were given 3 to 10 minutes to abandon ship with their belongings. The U-Boat only managed to sink seven out of a possible eighty boats in the Baltimore fleet. This was thanks to the appearance of a British patrol vessel, which caused the UC75 to submerge. The boats were scuttled by small bombs and, in one case, an engine in a Castletownsend boat was smashed by a large hammer. Thankfully no lives were lost but the fishermen were refused permission to take oars into their punts. When the U-Boat commander was challenged about this by a Cape Clear fisherman, who said: "I thought the Germans would do nothing to the Irish – that ye liked us."

The German replied sternly:

"Ah, my dear fellow, you don't know the Germans yet."

The German intimated that they had sunk all the Kinsale fishing boats en route to Baltimore and also the Waterford fishing fleet off Dunmore. They boasted that they would have every fishing boat at the bottom of the sea inside a month and then they would start shelling villages on the coast!

This threat caused consternation in the southern fishing communities and fuelled the propaganda war, which painted the Germans as the worst savages on earth and provided another valid excuse for the Americans to join in the fight against the evil Huns.

I could only find one incident where a U-Boat shelled the coast of Ireland. It happened on the North coast of Antrim at Port Ballintrae on Sunday 5th May 1918 when there was a shootout between the U-Boat U139 and the steamer WHEATEAR under the command of Captain David King. Neither ship was damaged during the two-and-a-half-hour exchange of gunfire. The only victim was an unfortunate cow hit by a stray shell!

The sinking of fishing vessels was common during this long war and there were attacks at Scarborough, Shetland and indeed incidents along the Irish coast already on record by May 1918. It certainly was not wise going to sea to fish for herring and mackerel with a lot of valuables in your pocket or without a lifebelt, life raft or punt of some sort. Insurance was also a priority given the fact that the U-Boats were becoming bolder and coming closer to the coast.

THE ATTACK OFF THE MOURNE COAST

The attack on the County Down fishing boats took place on the night of the 30th May 1918 and started between nine and ten o'clock. Half the fleet had gone south to Waterford, a traditional fishing ground at that time of year. The rest of the boats had just shot their drift nets about 12 to 14 miles out and were easy prey for Von Schrader's UB64. This U-Boat was a coastal torpedo attack class with a length of 180 feet and beam of 18 feet. It was usually crewed by 34 men who had 10 torpedoes and an 88-mm deck gun at their disposal. It could reach 13.6 knots on the surface and 8 knots submerged. More than enough speed to catch a steamer or fishing vessel on the run. Miles of nets were cast in the fishing grounds suspended from large floats or buoys and discs of cork with spring ropes at the bottom. The U-Boat could see the train of nets because each section of net had an inflated tarred canvas float called a pallet. They were waiting for the curtains to fill with nature's bounty and some of the boats were slinging lines overboard as well in an effort to haul in even bigger fish. The U-Boat came out of the mist dripping with water and one skipper realised why his compass had been spinning freely. After a few machine-gun bursts to grab their attention, they were asked if they were armed. Trapped by their nets, a German officer ordered them with megaphone in hand to: "Lay to and heave no line."

HEADING FOR THE FISHING GROUNDS

Once the Germans had established the boats were not members of the TRAWLER SECTION, scuttling charges (bombs about the size of a medium sized turnip) were made ready with long fuses. The Kilkeel and Annalong boats were the first targets and the crew of the NEVER CAN TELL had a very close encounter when they were rounded up and brought onto the U-Boat because they did not have a punt. On board the submarine, the enemy treated them kindly, with gin and cigarettes passed around. They were covered by armed ratings and a machine-gun at all times, but they were still at risk on deck. What would happen if a patrol boat suddenly appeared? The commander stated his intention to sink the fishing boats but also to use the MOSS ROSE as a lifeboat. Howard Forsythe told me that his grandfather, John McKee on board the MOSS ROSE, thought that initially the Germans were going to sink his boat and he shouted and cursed at them. He was addressed by megaphone in English to keep quiet and they would come to no harm. ** The MOSS ROSE was duly commandeered and the crew of the NEVER CAN TELL and other fishermen were put aboard this vessel. Charlie Cassidy pleaded in vain but his pride and joy CYPRUS was sent to a watery grave. The NEVER CAN TELL crew was transferred to the MOSS ROSE after one and a half hours on the deck of the UB64 as witnesses to the methodical destruction of the fishing boats. The small punts gathered around the MOSS ROSE and plans were made for the arduous slog for shore. At one point a member of a German boarding party was going to smash the engine of the MOSS ROSE but thankfully he changed his mind. The MOSS ROSE was ordered to keep behind the flotilla of punts and shepherd them safely to shore. Initially the engine of the good shepherd refused to kick into life and the punts drifted and rowed towards Kilkeel and safety. The sea was still calm but they were a long way out. After a lot of re-priming the engine eventually coughed into life and the little cockleshells and their escort limped towards the beach at Leestone. Family and friends in Kilkeel had no idea of the danger facing the hardy breadwinners.

NICKEY and NOBBY

It was 2.00 am before they reached shore and raised the alarm. The U-Boat then turned its attention to the Ardglass and Portavogie boats. Some of these boats managed to cut their nets and the ones with engines managed to escape to the north. Two boats from Portavogie, SEABIRD and GLAD TIDINGS, cut their herring nets in an effort to escape the U-Boat. After about 20 minutes they were overhauled by the superior speed of the enemy and small bombs were placed on board in what was now a standard routine. James Cully, Jim Young and John Young of Portavogie told me an interesting story about the GLAD TIDINGS in 2012. To gain a place on board this fishing boat in 1918, each fisherman had to supply his own nets. Five new nets had been shot near the boat and it was decided to try and save the new nets before attempting to escape the U-Boat. This delay proved costly and they were soon caught by the UB64. The bomber came aboard with the bomb in one hand and the long fuse draped around his neck like a necklace. The bomb was planted in the hold and sent the boat to the bottom. Apparently, the only thing taken by the Germans from this boat was a scrubbing brush! In the same incident recorded by Jim Blaney in 1982, Robert Young of the GLAD TIDINGS looked the U-Boat commander straight in the eye and asked him permission to return to his vessel to retrieve a pair of new boots from the hold! Permission was granted, and the men were allowed to row away in their punt. At the time of the sinking of the Portavogie boats, another Portavogie boat, the LEONORA with members of the Keenan family as crew, was ordered to take the crews ashore to Ardglass. Like the MOSS ROSE it acted as a lifeboat and saved the lives of the Portavogie crews and the crew of the MARIANNE McCRUM.

It was thought that the MARY JOSEPH had also been lost during these attacks, but she had been fishing elsewhere and missed out on all the excitement and destruction. She made a surprise but welcome return to the harbour a few days later.

Here is what was written by the skipper at the time: -

<u>NEVER CAN TELL - Statement of Master 6th July 1918</u>

On Thursday 30th May 1918 at 9 pm the NEVER CAN TELL was about 12 miles South by East from Kilkeel and was shooting her nets.

** Deponent saw a submarine about ¾ of a mile off heading South by East. The submarine veered round the nets, and after half an hour, fired 4 or 5 shots in the direction of the NEVER CAN TELL --- some across the bows and some around the quarter (stern). She then closed and John Donnan, one of Deponent's crew waved his coat to indicate that there was no yawl on the NEVER CAN TELL. The submarine approached still closer and Deponent's crew shouted that there was no yawl. Then an order came in good English to put up hands and get on the submarine, a man on the conning tower saying that if any of the other Fishing Boats were armed, all Deponent's crew would be shot. Deponent and his crew had then to proceed to the stern of the submarine and while so doing two of the submarine's crew went aboard the NEVER CAN TELL and bombed her, she sinking in 4 or 5 minutes. The submarine was 150-foot-long, slate coloured and black at the water line. The number was blotted out. Two guns were seen by Deponent --- a machine gun on the aft side of the conning tower and another gun about the same size as that on a coasting steamer forward. Deponent saw 8 or 9 men on the submarine but there were more below. They had no uniform just grey jerseys, different coloured trousers and 'Dutch Clogs'. Deponent heard some speak in English and others in another language which Deponent does not know.*

When the NEVER CAN TELL was sunk the submarine proceeded (with Deponent and crew) to the ST. MARY, CYPRUS, SPARKLING WAVE, HONEY BEE, in succession, sinking all with bombs. Next the MOSS ROSE was visited. This boat had no yawl and Deponent and his crew were ordered aboard her. A man on the conning tower saying at the same time, "TELL THEM ASHORE HOW

BAD WE WERE TO YOU, AND TELL THEM IN BELFAST WE WERE ASKING FOR THEM."

Deponent and crew were about 1 hour and 20 minutes on the submarine altogether. The MOSS ROSE with her crew and Deponent's crew landed at Kilkeel at about 2 am on the 31st May. None of the other nets or other gear was recovered. There were no confidential papers on board.

*Note Deponent refers to the Master or Skipper making the report.

The return from the MARIANNE McCRUM was also in some detail. Since this boat was sunk later, about 10.30 pm, it deserves to be read in full.

MARIANNE *McCRUM* Report of Master 5th July 1918

On Thursday 30th May at 9.30 pm the MARIANNE McCRUM was 14 miles SSW of Ardglass. Deponent had heard some shots previously. A submarine appeared over a mile off and approached to within a cable's length (200 yards). She then fired 4 or 5 shots across the MARIANNE McCRUM and veered to the starboard bow of the latter. An enquiry came from the submarine whether there was a small boat. Deponent answered "No", then another came to throw out a rope, which was made fast aft, and according to instructions Deponent and his crew boarded the submarine. Then the MARIANNE McCRUM was bombed and sank in a few minutes. This was about 10.30 pm. Deponent and his crew remained in the submarine until about 11 pm. Meanwhile the JANE GORDON and LLOYD were destroyed. Next a motor boat, name unknown from Portavogie, was reached and Deponent and crew were ordered thereon. Two more Portavogie boats were next sunk by the submarine and the crews picked up by the motor boat first mentioned. Deponent does not remember the names of the three motor boats.

(Author's Note: The two Portavogie boats sunk were SEABIRD and GLAD TIDINGS. The rescue vessel was the LEONORA from Portavogie.)

Deponent and his crew landed on the first mentioned motor boat at Ardglass at 3 am on the 31st May. Deponent did not see any number on the submarine which was of a greyish colour and about 120 feet long. Deponent heard only two of the submarine's crew speak English --- one of them who did the bombing did practically all the talking. He wanted to know whether any of the other fishing boats had guns or punts; also, the name and number of Deponent's boat. Deponent saw about 10 of the submarine's crew altogether --- most of them had greyish jerseys on and some had clogs. Deponent cannot state their nationality.

12 nets and 14 bulys(?) were recovered and restored to Deponent on 1st June, also 10 coils of spring rope on 2nd June. The former by two Government motor launches and the latter by a Patrol Boat. Some more gear was recovered but it is useless. Service was rendered by a motor boat from Portavogie. The rest of the gear is lost. There were no confidential papers on board.

The JANE GORDON was sunk about 11.00 pm 14 miles East Southeast from Kilkeel after the MARIANNE McCRUM had been blown up. The U-Boat came alongside and was estimated to be 150 feet long and apparently white coloured. About 15 men, including 7 from the MARIANNE McCRUM, were seen on deck. The skipper was ordered into his small punt and they rowed for shore. The German crew placed small bombs on board and sank the JANE GORDON. They then proceeded to the LLOYD from Annalong and sunk her in a similar fashion. The crew of the JANE GORDON in their small boat reached Kilkeel at 4.00 am on Friday morning. People in the town were still sleeping and did not realise that Fritz had dealt a deadly blow to the fishing trade of Mourne.

When the skipper of the SPARKLING WAVE heard and saw the sinking of the other boats he realised they had no chance to escape and he launched his small boat. In his own words, he wrote:

'We launched our small boat and commenced to pull towards the shore and when about ¼ of a mile away from our vessel the submarine went alongside and appeared to place bombs in the hold. The submarine left our vessel and shortly an explosion took place, about 5 minutes later the SPARKLING WAVE sank. We rowed the 12 miles to Ballymartin where we landed at 3.00 am on 31st May having lost the whole of our effects, also the ship's papers.'

James Donnan, Skipper of the QUEEN BEE, arrived late at the fishing grounds and missed all the excitement but he was able to tow some of the punts back safely to shore. Fortunately, he avoided the UB64 whilst on his rescue mission.

AFTERMATH

The sinking of the fishing boats quickly became the main topic of conversation in Kilkeel town and telegrams flew back and forth between Kilkeel and London. A Public Meeting was held to discuss the attack and to plan the way forward. Losses were estimated at £8,000 including the nets. The surviving Kilkeel and Annalong boats refused to return to the fishing grounds unless afforded protection by naval patrol boats. The Meeting represented the lives of 280 men in the tight knit fishing community and property valued at £40,000. A major recipient of the Post Office Telegraphs was the Earl of Kilmorey, Hyde Park Barracks, Knightsbridge, London since he was a major stakeholder in the Kilkeel fishing fleet and fishing industry. He was sent newspaper reports about the loss of the boats and urged to use his influence at the Admiralty to hasten patrol boats to the herring grounds. He was advised that a local crew could be 'got for a Patrol Boat if required'. He was also informed that two steam drifters had arrived on Saturday afternoon and proceeded to the fishing grounds where they managed to pick up most of the lost nets and some tackle.

Frank Chambers, Fish Merchant, who was in partnership with the Earl of Kilmorey, wrote to him on the 3rd June 1918 going into detail about the U-Boat attack and the role of the MOSS ROSE, which was one of their fishing boats. Again, Frank Chambers pushed for a patrol boat to guard the fleet and stressed that the fishing season was in jeopardy now, because the fishermen refused to go to sea unless protection was given to their vessels.

Frank Chambers referred specifically to their fishing boat MOSS ROSE, which was involved in the rescue of the fishermen:

" It was a very lucky job he did not break the MOSS ROSE engine. He was going to and then changed his mind."

The MOSS ROSE had to leave its nets behind but went out on Saturday and saved part of them. He lost 17 nets but Frank said they were insured and he had more in reserve for the fishing season. Frank, always the businessman, hoped 'it would not be long until we have a patrol for the fleet.' To sugar the pill, he added:

" The CONSTANCE had a fine shot (catch) in Dunmore East last week of £179 and from the past two weeks £280 and MAID grossed £170 for two weeks."

These were boats operated by the two men. Colonel Sir James Craig MP and Mr. J. MacVeagh MP were also lobbied by the Ardglass fishermen to use their influence to obtain protection for their fishing boats.

It was not until 21st June 1918 that official word was received from the Admiralty that arrangements had been made for patrol vessels - WHENEVER AVAILABLE - to cruise among the fishing fleets. Nonetheless, fishing activity was disrupted for two weeks but helped by pressure from the Earl of Kilmorey, 2 armed protection vessels were sent to the fishing grounds.

THE PROPAGANDA WAR

At this time the media, mostly newspapers and wireless transmissions, were subject to censorship and the candid reports of 1915 when U-Boat attacks were a novelty, were replaced by accounts by writers who were schooled in the arts of deception and misinformation, in an effort to influence the thought processes of the Irish public. In the background to all reports was the propaganda war against the Irish attitude to the Germans, the fallout from German support for the 1916 Rising, the Recruiting Drive in Ireland and the issue of Conscription here and Germany.

GERMAN SUBMARINE SINKS
COUNTY DOWN FISHING BOATS!
MEN OF COUNTY DOWN! ARE YOU GOING TO PERMIT THIS!
BE REVENGED BY JOINING
THE TRAWLER SECTION, ROYAL NAVAL RESERVE!
AGE 18 TO 50
PAY 3s 8d per day,
with 1s 8d extra for food allowance when serving afloat

The sinking of the fishing boats was a gift for the propaganda merchant and the Admiralty very soon had notices placarded around the ports of County Down exhorting young men to join the TRAWLER SECTION. The TRAWLER SECTION was designed to recruit Irishmen between 18 and 50. The pay varied according to the brand of service. For example, a stoker (18 to 38 years old) received 11s 8d per week plus free kit, rations, separation allowance and 1s 8d in lieu of rations when afloat. Candidates could enrol at any Irish Recruiting Office. In the Auxiliary Patrol Section with steam trawlers and drifters, the men would have been involved in Mine Sweeping duties and Mine Laying. In other words, not only clearing the sea-lanes, but sowing the seeds of destruction as well. Other recruits were involved in coaling the destroyers from colliers working winches, bagging coal and loading the bunker chutes to feed the engine room.

NEWSPAPER APPEAL

The Belfast Evening Telegraph on 4th June 1918 made a special appeal for the plight of the fishermen. The newspaper highlighted the fact that a lot of men *indeed have been - probably many of them were - pro-German in their sympathies but the bitter experience of Friday night May 31st has changed it all and they are to-day as anti-German as the best Briton born. The value of the 17 boats sunk is roughly estimated at between £6,500 and £8,000.'*

This article is highly suspect and its source was a Skibereen correspondent who could hardly have had first-hand access to the men and their political leanings.

By the 5th July 1918, Mr. William Johnston, the solicitor from Newry, came to Kilkeel to address the owners and crews of the fishing boats sunk by the U-Boat. He gave advice to them about seeking compensation from the German government and quoted The Hague Convention several times. He urged the fishermen to lodge their claims with the proper Government Department and called upon the Government to enforce payment of those claims out of the war indemnity fund. His main thrust was that Germany should be made to pay. He also was keen to recruit men for the war effort and pointed out that some local men had joined the TRAWLER SECTION.

OTTO VON SCHRADER

There is no doubt that Von Schrader was kind and polite to the fishermen on board the submarine. He doled out drinks and cigarettes and ensured that the MOSS ROSE and LEONORA were used as lifeboats to ferry the men safely to shore. This is verified by the official documentation written by the men involved at the time.

In the First World War, he was a very successful U-Boat commander and credited with sinking 57 ships. He was well decorated by the Kaiserliche Marine with an Iron Cross 1st Class by August 1916. He started off with the rank of Oberleutnant Zur See and, by April 1917, he was promoted to Kapitänleutnant. He was a courageous commander and took considerable risks when attacking the troopship JUSTICA on the 19th July 1918. The JUSTICA built by Harland and

Wolff was one of the biggest ships torpedoed during the war at 32,234 tons. Von Schrader was operating in a wolf pack at this time and braved the escorts accompanying the outbound convoy. There were seven destroyers acting as escort but despite this the UB64 got close enough to score a direct hit which brought the big ship to a standstill. He was subjected to a heavy rain of depth charges for two hours and then returned for another attack. He missed and the depth charges descended again. He survived the onslaught and three hours later returned for another attack which failed to sink the crippled liner. The next day, when the liner was on tow, she was attacked by the UB124 and finally sunk by two torpedoes NNW of Inishtrahill. The UB64 was surrendered on the 21st November 1918 and broken up at Fareham.

Von Schrader continued his naval career into the Second World War and acquired more decorations such as a Clasp to the Iron Cross in 1940 and the Knight's Cross of the Iron Cross in 1943. In the Kriegsmarine, he reached the rank of Admiral in charge of the Norwegian West Coast. It was in the late stages of the war that he made his biggest mistake, which branded him a war criminal. Von Schrader was now a member of the Nazi War Machine and this indoctrination may have corroded his humanity and sense of decency that was evident in the First World War. In 1943, Von Schrader's forces off the west coast of Norway captured a British torpedo boat with a British crew in British uniforms. These men became prisoners of war and should have been treated as such under International Law. Von Schrader, following directives from Hitler, handed them over to the Sicherheitsdienst (SD, Security Service) who, adhering to Hitler's Commando Order executed them and disposed of their bodies at sea. At the end of the war, Von Schrader was arrested for war crimes and committed suicide on the 19th July 1945 in Bergen. He is buried in his Prussian birthplace, Lyck (Elk) now in Poland north of Warsaw.

SOURCES OF INFORMATION

1 'My Mourne' By J S Doran, 1974 Mourne Observer Press
The Tale of the Never Can Tell

2 'Sailing Ships of Mourne' By W. J. Fitzpatrick 1995
Revised Edition Mourne Observer Press

3 12 Miles of Mourne - Volume 9 - 2010
Telling the Tale of the Never Can Tell by Ian Taylor

4 Journal of the Upper Ards Historical Society Number 6 1982
The Great War and the Upper Ards by Jim Blaney

5 National Archives Kew ADM 137/4017

6 Larne Times 2nd June 1917
'Irish Fishing Boats Sunk 1917'

7 Mourne Observer 16th November 1962
'The Sinking of the Fleet'
A Poem by J S Doran from facts supplied by Jimmy Collins, The Moor, Kilkeel and possibly John Collins and Charlie Cassidy

8 Mourne Observer 18th June 2008
Why did a German Submarine Captain show such compassion to fishermen from Mourne? By Ian Taylor

9 Down Recorder Saturday 8th June 1918
'Down Herring Fleet Raided'

10 Northern Whig 3rd June 1918

11 Belfast News Letter 3rd June 1918; 12th June 1918

12 Irish Times 12th June 1918.
The Sinking of Irish Fishing Boats

13 Belfast Evening Telegraph 4th June; 5th June; 6th June;
8th June; 10th June; 29th June 1918

14 Irish Times 4th June 1918 Letter to the Editor

15 New York Times 15th June 1918
Submarine Destroys Irish Fishing Fleet

16 Public Record Office NI Kilkeel Fishing Boats
D2638/D/100/1-8; Compensation COM/43/1/1; CUS/3/5/1; CUS/3/6/3/1

17 Down Recorder 3rd November 1918

18 u.boat.net

19 British Vessels Lost at Sea 1914 -1918

20 Library Staff in the Newspaper Library & Central Library Belfast, Downpatrick & Newry Library

21 Edward Robinson, Harbour Master, Portavogie; James Cully, Jim Young & John Young Portavogie 2012

** **AUTHOR'S NOTE**

There is a persistent rumour in the Kilkeel fishing community that the German U-Boat commander had visited the town before the outset of war and that this was his reason for ensuring that no lives were lost on any of the fishing boats. One story relates that he was a bandsman who stayed with a Mrs Quinn on the Mountain Road in 1912. Another story says that he stayed with a Mrs Collins on the Mountain Road. There was a Mrs. Collins on the Mountain Road and she ran a guesthouse with her two daughters. Howard Forsythe told me that his grandfather was spoken to personally by the German Commander and that he gave the impression he knew him before the war. He told Captain McKee to stop shouting abuse and that he was going to use the MOSS ROSE as a lifeboat. Apparently, there was a letter in the Mourne Observer several years ago from a German lady who was trying to verify the story. So far, I can find no concrete evidence that Von Schrader was in Kilkeel before the war. There were about 30 men on the U-Boat and one of the officers may have made a visit before the war but proving that fact is a different matter.

NOBBY

Hugh went to sea when he was 17 years old and gained his basic training as an Ordinary Seaman (OS) on the barque, ANTRIM, out of Liverpool. By April 1886, he was an Able Seaman (AB) on the SS CASPIAN and SS PERUVIAN of the Allan line based at 18, James Street, Liverpool. There were transatlantic crossings to Canada and the U.S.A. with passengers on board. By 1891 he switched to sail power and worked for two years out of South Wales on the DUNBOYNE. Captain John O'Neill, his cousin, was the Master of this large sailing ship registered at 1,380 tons.

THE DUNBOYNE

The DUNBOYNE was a big sailing ship that looked like a tea clipper in terms of sail layout. Her hull was made of iron at Whitehaven in 1888 and she was owned by Sir Richard Martin, who registered the vessel in Dublin. His address was given as 29 Sir John Rogerson's Quay, Dublin This big ship was registered at 1,425 gross tons and 1,380 net tons when Hugh O'Neill was on board from 1891 to 1893. She was classed as A1 on her last inspection at Liverpool and her dimensions were 243.1 feet long by 37.5 feet wide and 21.5 feet deep. Three great masts carried 15 square sails with triangular sails rigged fore and aft. Her call sign was KRDP and Hugh would have learned early on from Captain John O'Neill, how to signal a passing vessel with the four flags which spelt out these letters. Anne Howard, an expert on the O'Neill family tree, drew my attention to a book called: *'Dear Daughter' ~ The Messenger Letters 1890 – 1898*, which has an interesting section on the DUNBOYNE. The Letters were written by Thomas Messenger, the Mate on the ship at this time. He wrote on a regular basis to his young daughter, Mary Adelaide, who lived at Crosby near Maryport, Cumbria. Hugh O'Neill was on board during the long voyage to South Australia and back. Thanks to the Messenger Letters, we can build up a picture of what life was like for the young Hugh, especially when they are read in conjunction with the official ship's log.

John O'Neill had been accompanied by Thomas Messenger and James O'Neill on a long voyage to Portland (Oregon) from Antwerp on the 24th July 1890. They were away almost a year before the voyage terminated at Hull on the 22nd June 1891. Hugh O'Neill did not join the DUNBOYNE until the 10th August 1891. He had left the PERUVIAN and was rated an Able Seaman (AB) with a monthly wage of £3 10s 0d. His first voyage was from Sunderland to Port Pirie, South Australia. Details of this voyage are sparse in the logbook and there is more to be gained by concentrating on his second voyage thanks to the Messenger Letters.

Dunboyne Sailing Ship

city at Port Pirie, with their improvised chimneys made from kerosene cans. There were other temptations and five of the crew deserted ship.

By December 1892, there was only some pig iron left to unload and then the prospect of loading a cargo of wheat at Port Pirie and Wallaroo. Messenger received letters and papers from his daughter in Crosby, which told him about the hard frost back home and the freezing of the River Thames. Mrs O'Neill stayed ashore during the loading process and the baby put on weight and started to wave and say 'Ta'.

The young men on board had a good time ashore at Wallaroo with plenty of 'local sheilas' attracted by the peak caps and flash of buttons. The five deserters had to be hurriedly replaced by other seamen on the 21st January 1893. The return journey was planned for Queenstown, and Messenger predicted 100 days at sea. John O'Neill brought a kangaroo on board as a pet! There was also the novelty of a whistling parrot, pups and chickens. This zoo collection probably helped to break up the monotony of long days at sea.

By February, the DUNBOYNE had crossed the Pacific to Seattle. Mrs O'Neill slipped on some ice on deck as she was heading for Mass. John O'Neill was also unwell and the cold, snow and frost did not help matters. There are large gaps in the record of the return journey and Messenger does not mention the death by drowning of Thomas Morgan AB who was washed overboard on the 21st February 1893. This occurred in the midst of a heavy gale when it was impossible to launch a rescue boat. There is no mention of the dangerous Cape Horn route that must have tested the courage and mettle of Hugh O'Neill.

In March 1893, the DUNBOYNE also rescued survivors from the sailing ship TEMPLEMORE that had been crushed by massive icebergs east of the Falkland Islands. John O'Neill landed the grateful survivors at Port Stanley.

Hugh O'Neill was discharged in London on the 25th May 1893 with an extra £23 8s 4d in his pockets and a wealth of experience on a tall ship and stories to tell of his voyages around the Cape of Good Hope and Cape Horn; using the SE and NE Trade Winds. John O'Neill was an experienced mariner and helped

Hugh acquire the skills on board this big square-rigged ship. John O'Neill stayed with the ship until 1904. On his next voyage out from England, Baby O'Neill took ill and despite careful nursing by the parents, Anne Mabel died at sea. She was only 14 months old and Messenger describes the painful burial at sea. The baby was placed in a wooden coffin, which was wrapped in a length of chain to make it sink. Kathleen was grief stricken and placed a diamond ring in the coffin. The baby featured on a regular basis in Messenger's letters and he painted a sombre picture of the dead infant and the unusual burial at sea.

John O'Neill returned to Killowen in 1910, after his father died. He became a Justice of the Peace and represented Killowen on the Kilkeel Rural District Council and Board of Guardians. He was killed in an unfortunate motorcycle accident near Narrow Water on the 28th October 1920.

The DUNBOYNE has lasted to this day and was sold on to Norway and then to the Swedish Navy as a sail training ship in 1923. Her name was changed to AF CHAPMAN and in 1949 she was anchored in Stockholm Harbour. At the time of writing in 2012, she is still afloat and serving as a youth hostel for the Swedish Tourist Association. There are many pictures of the ship on the Internet just the click of a button away.

Keen to build on his experience at sea, Hugh passed his exam for Second Mate in July 1893 and then joined the SS CASOS back in Liverpool where he served as a Second Mate for four months up to February 1895. He still had a desire to improve and sat his First Mate exams in April 1895. Soon after he became First Mate on the barquentine named SKODA of Windsor, Nova Scotia. His training on the DUNBOYNE helped him in the running of this sailing ship. All these voyages on different vessels helped him to prepare his logbook and in 1896 he passed his exam for a Master's ticket while in Belfast. He switched to steamers in 1897 and worked on the SS CUMERIA and SS ARAUCANIA up to 1899. There were long voyages to South America and the east coast of the U.S.A. Hugh then signed on for a three year spell on the SS WERNETH HALL with voyages to Canada, Cape Colonies, West Africa and U.S.A.

the eastern seaboard of the U.S.A. From April 1909, Hugh made voyages to Genoa, Taganrog (Sea of Azov), Rotterdam and Barry, South Wales. There were lengthy voyages to Piraeus in Greece, Braila and Galatz on the Danube delta and then back to Antwerp in Belgium. The cargo was mostly coal, as there were warnings about taking naked lights or lighting matches in the holds below decks. The coal was usually loaded from the South Wales coalfield and grain was the main cargo on the return journey to European ports. He seems to have been paid at £11 per month for acting as Mate and dealing with a cosmopolitan crew from places like Dundalk, King's Lynn, Cardiff, Redditch, Greece, Turkey and Albania.

A sample of his 1909 voyages includes: -

1	7th October 1909	Barry, South Wales
2	19th October 1909	Spezia, North Italy
3	6th November 1909	Braila, Danube
4	10th December 1909	Antwerp, Belgium

In 1910, he was still Mate on this ship and paid at the same rate. He sailed from Barry or Newport probably with coal to destinations like Port Said in Egypt, Odessa in Russia, Bremen in Germany, Genoa, Berdiansk in the Ukraine, the River Danube and back to Antwerp. He was away at sea for most of the time and this must have put a strain on family life.

ON THE SS DUNDALK

Hugh left the ULIDIA in January 1911 and joined the Dundalk and Newry Steam Packet Company later in July 1911. He sailed initially on the SS BESSBROOK, which operated out of Newry. She had been built at Pointhouse, Glasgow by A. & J. Inglis as a single screw steamer in 1877. There was accommodation for 30 First Class passengers and livestock. Iron built, she was 182 feet long by 27 feet wide and 14 feet deep. She had Thomas Jones, a loyal member of the company, as Managing Owner. The BESSBROOK was a reliable workhorse for the company and remained in service until 1928.

Hugh was the Mate on the BESSBROOK and he worked with Patrick Quinn as Master and another 16 crewmembers. Alfred Hill was the 1st Engineer, William Tuite a Fireman, John Higgins an Able Seaman, John Hearty a Winchman, Patrick Creegan a Steward and Annie Creegan a Stewardess. These were some of the crew on board. Hugh was paid at £2 0s 0d per week and the ship was principally engaged between Dundalk, Newry, Liverpool and Ardrossan carrying passengers, livestock and general cargo. The crew was very stable up to January 1912 and then, because of strike action; there was more turbulence and transfers to other ships in the fleet.

By the 18th February 1912, Hugh O'Neill had joined the SS DUNDALK as First Mate with John Berrill from Drogheda as Master. His pay had risen slightly to £2 5s 0d per week. This was not a good time for the company because of strike action by the crews of the DUNDALK and BESSBROOK over a matter of discipline. When this problem was resolved, a foot and mouth outbreak and a coal strike disrupted sailings for a time.

An even greater problem occurred on the 22nd March 1912 when the DUNDALK was approaching the Mersey. She ran aground on the West Hoyle Bank and there was an anxious time for the company before she was successfully refloated on a high tide on Sunday 31st March 1912.

Mr S. J. Cocks, the General Manager, ran back and forth to Liverpool to oversee the salvage operation with the crew and consulting engineers, Martin & Sinclair. First, they had to rescue the cattle and then lighten the ship. Then two tugs were brought in to tow her into deep water. An inspection showed there was no serious damage, but the cost of the salvage operation amounted to £1,886 3s 10d. This did not go down well with the shareholders in the company since the cost had to be taken from the Reserve Fund.

Following this incident, Captain Berrill resigned from the company after 41 years of service. He did not receive a pension but was given a £300 gratuity instead. He left the ship on the 29th April 1912 and Hugh took over as Acting Captain from the same date. Patrick Quinn from Dundalk became the 1st Mate. Berrill was recognised as a bluff old salt and a true gentleman. He died in Liverpool on the 2nd October 1920.

In the aftermath of the TITANIC disaster in April 1912, Hugh and the crew were affected by new Board of Trade regulations regarding lifeboats, lifeboat drill and life-saving appliances. Later in June 1912, an outbreak of foot and mouth disease in Ireland halted the export of livestock. S. J. Cocks at Dundalk and John Stokes (Newry Agent) were on the lookout for alternative cargoes to keep the company solvent and Hugh gainfully employed. Sometime in 1912, Hugh moved to the Quay Cottage, Rostrevor and he was now the Master of the SS DUNDALK.

A truly bizarre and mysterious incident happened to the SS DUNDALK on Sunday 27th April 1913, which must have puzzled Hugh as well. The ship had sunk in Stanley Dock, Liverpool. As a consequence of a Board of Trade Survey, the ship had arrived in the dock the week before for a complete overhaul. A policeman, on foot patrol, at 4.00 am spotted the ship sinking and sounded the alarm. The 20 crew were roused from their sleep and, accompanied by the ship's cat and kittens, evacuated the vessel which gradually sank. She listed over to her port side and lay almost on her beam ends. It was thought that a seacock had been left open.

Another delicate and expensive salvage operation was required to right the ship. Chains were placed under the hull, then 'camels' to right her and finally the pumping out of seawater. The Reserve Account was drained of another £1,407 18s 8d. Later in June 1913, the Company concluded that the sinking was a malicious act and a reward of £50 was offered for information. The Chairman, T. Callan Macardle and S. J. Cocks, General Manager, still described the incident as 'mysterious' in September 1913.

1914 started off well for the Dundalk and Newry Steam Packet Company; largely because of trade disturbances in Dublin Port which restricted services from Dublin for about three months. This brought new traffic to Dundalk and helped to offset the increased expenditure on coal supplies, wages and harbour dues. A new Tonnage Act had come into operation on 1st January 1914 and costs were expected to rise by £1,000 per annum in the Mersey. Hugh was now living in Park Street, Dundalk within easy reach of the docks.

After another foot and mouth outbreak, Dundalk Harbour opened again for the shipment of beef and two large shipments were sent to Birkenhead at the end of March 1914. Newry was still closed at this stage for trade in livestock and this presented a mystery to the Company given that Belfast and Dundalk were open for business and drawing on the same catchment.

Spare cash was invested wisely in reliable stocks such as the Great Northern Railway in order to make some profit to help pay for higher insurance rates on the ships. They did not realise that they were steadily creeping towards one of the bloodiest conflicts ever seen on the planet.

When the war started, the SS DUNDALK carried on with its normal trade across the Irish Sea. The Company Chairman, T. Callan Macardle, stated: 'that we are able to carry on our business with a certain degree of comfort due to our army and navy, which up to the present has enabled us to cross and recross the Irish

Sea with the utmost degree of safety.' Nobody could have foreseen that the SS DUNDALK was to encounter two U-Boats in the Irish Sea in 1917 and 1918. The foot and mouth outbreaks of 1912 and February 1914 had led to changes in the shipment of livestock from Ireland. There were tighter controls in place and the ships had to sail for lairages at Birkenhead, where accommodation was limited causing delays for the captains like Hugh O'Neill. A big advantage for the Company was the fact that competitors for the Irish Sea trade had had their ships commandeered by the Admiralty and War Office. This created a rush of traffic and healthy profits initially. The shareholders were rubbing their hands with glee.

However, when the U21 entered the Irish Sea in January 1915 and sank the KILCOAN and other ships, the situation changed quite dramatically and merchant seamen realised that they were in grave danger. The Company was shaken out of its aura of complacency and thought it prudent to insure all the fleet against War Risks. All employees were granted a War Bonus in addition to their ordinary wage. Coal supplies were erratic and it was difficult to get a steady supply because of the war effort. The market value of investments had fallen steadily and the Company thought it could make a case for encouraging pig breeding in Ireland with an eye to bigger profit margins in the future.

By October 1915, the Company showed a loss because of the diminution of trade. The U-Boats had frightened off the passenger traffic. There were wage problems as well, mostly on the Newry vessels. The SS DUNDALK largely escaped the wage problem but, shortly after the U21 attacks, the crew refused to go to sea because they were afraid that they would not be able to launch the lifeboats or survive in the event of a torpedo attack during the rough seas at the time. They went to sea the next day but this incident shows the real stress they were under. Hugh and Samuel J. Cocks, General Manager, tried to deal with all staff concerns and the Chairman thanked the sailors and firemen for their loyalty.

There was another incident in the crowded Mersey involving the DUNDALK and another vessel, the SS LESTRIS, from the Cork Steamship Company on Sunday the 24th October 1915. No serious damage was incurred in the collision between the two vessels, but the DUNDALK was laid up for a week while an after gangway was repaired. Later in March 1916, the owners of the LESTRIS decided to sue the Dundalk and Newry Steam Packet Company for damages arising out of the collision. The defendants, denying responsibility, counterclaimed for damages. The accident happened in the Wallesey Stage of the Mersey and the final judgement was that both parties were to blame. Judgement was made in favour of the LESTRIS for a moiety of their claim but no costs.
The Company continued to be faced with increased expenses under four main headings:

War Risks on all steamers was running at £1,262 every six months.
War Bonus to staff was granted at 6s per week and this was given to shore workers as well to meet the extra cost of living.
Coal Prices had risen again by at least 50%.
Repairs to the steamers were now more expensive because of Admiralty priorities.

In March 1916, there were strong rumours that the Company was going to be sold. The Council called a meeting to assess the impact of such a sale on the town of Dundalk. Trade, employment, harbour dues, transport and shops would all be affected in a negative spiral of decline. This was a worry for all the sailors and their families. There was a palpable sense of relief when the Company and shareholders looked to the long-term future of Dundalk and the rumoured sale was put on hold. Newry seemed to present more trouble for the Company than Dundalk. There were problems with the ships scraping the bottom of the Newry canal and pinpricking labour disputes, which resulted in a loss of business. The 1916 Rising led to political tensions with the Chairman coming down in favour of Kitchener and the Empire. Understandable, since his sons, Lieutenant Kenneth Callan Macardle and Lieutenant John Ross Macardle were fighting on the front line. Kenneth was killed in the battle for Trones Wood on the 9th July 1916.

The SS IVEAGH had to be put out to charter because of a Government prohibition on the sale of potatoes and oats to the mainland. These were reliable cargoes for the English and Scottish markets between November and June. Despite all the setbacks and thanks to Hugh and all the crew on the flagship vessel, the SS DUNDALK, the Company was able to report in 1918 a gain in profits and 'a most satisfactory year.' Freight rates had been increased during the war and this enabled the Company to stay in business, pay a decent dividend, plan for the future and pay the sailors and firemen a fair wage in line with the rest of the shipping companies around the Irish Sea. The weekly wage of seamen and firemen had now reached £3 17s 6d. The Reserve Fund was now in a healthy state and the old EARL OF ERNE had been sold to a Greek firm with a delivery planned when peace was declared.

Captain  Hugh O'Neill

14th OCTOBER 1918

Samuel John Cocks from Liverpool was a very efficient and competent General Manager of the Company who was also a member of the Dundalk Harbour Board. He was a stickler for detail in meetings, especially where financial matters were concerned. He always fought for the good of the Company, shareholders and workforce by trying to gain the best deal. On the night of 14th

October 1918, he was the only passenger listed on the return journey from Liverpool to Dundalk, having just attended his brother's funeral in Flintshire. He had been manager of the company for ten years and had an intimate knowledge of shipping and railway matters gained from the London and North-Western Railway Company (Dublin, North Wall). His management skills helped the company thrive. In the Harbour Board meetings, he proved a valuable member and managed to ruffle a few feathers. Like Hugh O'Neill and crew, he risked his life many times in crossing the Irish Sea on business and visiting his family in Liverpool. On this October night, the steamer was carrying 150 tons of general cargo. Also on board were the remains of a Warrenpoint man, Patrick Hanratty, who had died in Liverpool of influenza. In 1918, an influenza epidemic had swept through the country resulting in a great loss of life. A DUNDALK crewmember, he had left the ship on health grounds only five days earlier. His body was being carried home for interment in Dundalk.

The SS DUNDALK left Collinwood Dock, Liverpool at 5.00 pm and headed northwest on her regular course between Anglesey and the Isle of Man, intending to reach the docks at Dundalk by early morning.

U90

The U90 had approached the Irish Sea target area from the North of Scotland and, by the 10th October 1918, this U-Boat commanded by Kapitänleutnant Heinrich Jess was north of Donegal and west of Islay. He steered South East via the North Channel and started to hunt merchant ships between the Isle of Man and the Skerries. On the 13th October, he failed on one torpedo attack and was depth charged by a U-Boat hunter which fired 4 depth charges. Three aircraft and two airships arrived over his dive position and searched until evening. 72 depth charges were dropped but none were close to the U-Boat. The U90 headed towards Liverpool Bay on the evening of the 14th October and spotted a large steamer, zig zagging on a 290^0 course. An escort steamer had turned back after an hour and the U-Boat reached a forward position around 12 midnight (German Time). It was a bright moonlit night with clear visibility and she dived for attack. The commander shot Numbers 3 and 4 torpedoes (a double shot) because of the distance involved. They were set at 4 and 5 metres depth for the 900 metre run towards the steamer, the SS DUNDALK.

Shortly after 11.00 pm, the Dundalk steamer was NNW of Anglesey when one of the torpedoes exploded. Captain Hugh O'Neill was on the starboard side of the bridge, having just relieved the Mate, John Higgins. The torpedo hit the SS DUNDALK amidships on the port side and practically split the steamer in two. The steamer began to sink immediately with the loss of twenty people.

THE SHOOTOUT OF DECEMBER 1917

Captain Hugh O'Neill and the SS DUNDALK had encountered a U-Boat before on the 6th December 1917. By sailing at full steam ahead and using a zigzag course (see diagram) he managed to outrun and outmanoeuvre the submarine despite being shelled by the latter's deck gun.

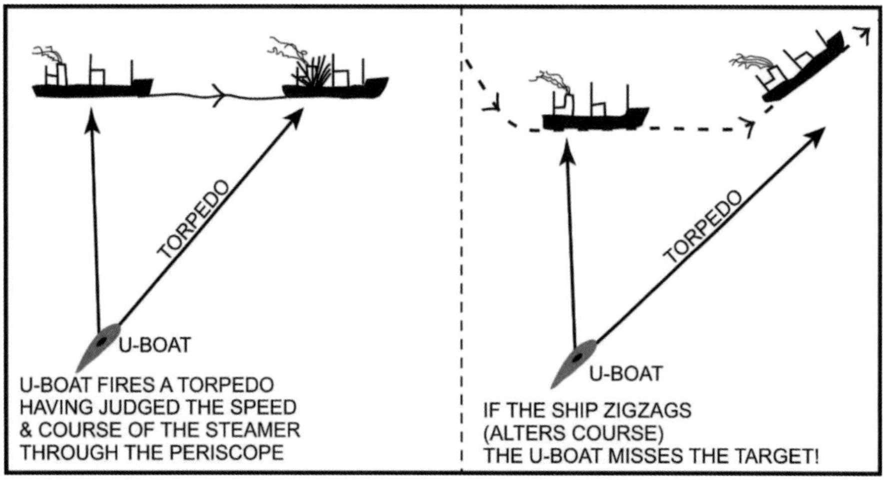

Zigzag evasion technique

The DUNDALK had left Liverpool at 3.00 am and followed a course for Dundalk as advised by Naval Intelligence. When south of the Calf of Man, the Mate spotted a vessel at 10 am, about 5 miles distant. The Mate realized it was a U-Boat when it was off the port quarter of the steamer and a shell was fired from the deck gun. The DUNDALK raised her speed to 14 knots and tried to keep the enemy astern. Captain O'Neill headed North East for the Isle of Man, zig zagging to avoid the deck gun shells. About 52 shells were fired at the steamer but there was only one direct hit on a lifeboat, which was blown to pieces. The ship's gunners returned fire from their 90mm deck gun but the rounds fell short of the target. One report suggests that the SS DUNDALK deck gun was a left over from the Boer War. This shootout lasted an hour and a half before the SS DUNDALK reached a safe zone at the Isle of Man. Hugh O'Neill escaped by using short zig zags and throwing 6 smoke boxes overboard to upset the aim of the German gunners. When the next batch of smoke boxes failed to ignite, the steamer made its own smoke which hid the ship from view. Gradually, the DUNDALK began to outrun the U90 and reached safety at Peel on the Isle of Man.

Captain O'Neill, his chief engineer Edward Johnston, and crew of trusty stokers and gunners had saved the flagship of the company as well as the livelihoods of those on board by skilful seamanship and courage. On Thursday 21st March 1918, in the Boardroom of the Steam Packet Company, a presentation was made to Captain O'Neill, officers and crew of the SS DUNDALK. Mr T. Callan Macardle, D.L., Chairman of the Company, supported by a full meeting of directors and Mr Samuel J. Cocks, Manager, made the presentation. A monetary reward and warm expression of appreciation was received from the Ministry of Shipping in recognition of the bravery of the crew. There was also a letter from Lloyd's forwarding a sum of money in addition to that awarded by the Ministry of Shipping and the bonus from the company. Lloyd's also made a proposal to give Captain O'Neill Lloyd's Silver Medal for meritorious service on 6th December 1917.

on, some of the CARLINGFORD crew noticed wreckage on the sea north of Anglesey and heard cries in the dark. The CARLINGFORD did ease up and circle to look for survivors but, given the fate of the LEINSTER and now the DUNDALK, thought it too dangerous to linger in the vicinity lest they go the same way. The U-Boat was probably on the surface when they passed the scene of the carnage. They had spotted lifeboats and heard cries for help and this news was reported at Dundalk Harbour. Their report caused distressing scenes at the Steam Packet offices as families and friends gathered to find out further details. Had the crew escaped on the lifeboats? One or two lifeboats could have carried the whole crew but exact numbers were imprecise.

The actions of the crew of the SS CARLINGFORD on the night of the sinking caused controversy in the town and led to families being split in the aftermath. It was a difficult dilemma for the SS CARLINGFORD since the Admiralty instructions were quite clear:

'No ocean-going British Merchant vessel is permitted to go to the assistance of a ship which has been torpedoed by a submarine.'

Perhaps when one studies: --

HOME WATERS TELEGRAM No.823 Dated 15/10/18 and sent out at 9.52 am, it may help explain the actions of the SS CARLINGFORD.

Following received from Customs, Dundalk begins: --

> *Master Hughes, SS CARLINGFORD reports when in position 18 miles North by West of the Skerries at 23.45 pm, October 14th, sighted 2 ships boats full of men. After making an effort to pick up survivors, observed conning tower of submarine – effort abandoned and proceeded on voyage (to Dundalk).*

Telegrams were sent off to the Welsh Harbour Authorities but there was no news forthcoming early on Tuesday morning.

It was not until 11.00 pm on Tuesday night that the first positive signs that there were survivors came through via telegram from Holyhead. The Admiralty trawler STORMCOCK had landed seven members of the crew there. The distress and anxiety continued because no names were given.

At 3.00 am on Wednesday another telegram arrived stating that five of the crew had been rescued by the SS DOUGLAS and landed safely in the Isle of Man. The rest of the crew were missing presumed lost. Only one name, J. Mulqueen, had been relayed to the company offices, a fact which caused more distress among the families holding vigil on the dockside.

SS DUNDALK (from the official report)

This 794 gross tons steamer was torpedoed without warning and sunk while on a voyage from Liverpool to Dundalk on 14th October 1918. She was owned by the Dundalk and Newry Steam Packet Company and carried a general cargo of 150 tons on board with 27 crew, 4 cattlemen and 1 passenger.
The vessel was attacked at 11 pm 5 miles NNW of the Skerries, Anglesey and sank immediately. The torpedo struck amidships on the portside. The mate got away with another man in one of the small boats and picked up five others. *They saw the submarine about 10 yards from the lifeboat, but the enemy went off. These men were rescued by Stormcock. Two seamen floated off the sinking ship on a raft and picked up the 2nd Engineer and a Fireman. These men were picked up by the S.S. Douglas.*
21 lives were lost including the Master. 7 men were picked up by Stormcock and landed at Holyhead.
4 men were picked up by S.S. Douglas and landed at Douglas.

[There are some errors in this report ~ 20 lives were lost including the Master Hugh O'Neill and the Manager Samuel J. Cocks, the SS DOUGLAS saved 5 lives. The wreck site, found by Isle of Man divers, is also further north and lies about halfway between the Skerries and the southern tip of the Isle of Man (about 18 miles SSW of Langness on the southern tip of the Isle of Man). This report only gives a bare outline of what really happened.]

THE LIFEBOATS

From the survivors, an account of what happened was gradually built up. The torpedo had exploded in the engine room on the port side. Staff in the engine room were probably killed instantly and those in their berths had little chance of survival. For some of the crew, like Harold Grey from Swansea, this was their first ship and again lifeboat drill would not have been second nature. He had only joined the SS DUNDALK on the 15th June 1918. John Higgins, the Acting 1st Mate, and Patrick Byrne managed to scramble into a lifeboat which had been struck by the main derrick. The lifeboat, which was floating at this stage, was cut free and although it was badly damaged and half-full of water they pulled five other survivors aboard. The ship went down within five minutes. Captain Hugh O'Neill was last seen on the bridge which had been blown up in the explosion. Darkness, dust and cinders obscured the visibility for the survivors. The men in the water cried for help as the ship went down fast. Higgins hauled Frank Deery, Patrick Kearney and James Tuite from the water.

These men were extremely lucky as they had been in the deck cabin. Tuite had been the most fortunate as he had gone down with the ship and then blasted back to the surface in a mass of air bubbles. Angus Ferguson, a gunner from Stornoway, was a very sick man and he was found floating on a hatch cover clad only in his under clothes. He was another flu victim and the ship had already lost a lot of its regular crew to the epidemic.

Timothy Connor, another gunner from Cork, was found clinging to a cattle board. Connor had been on gun duty and was dressed in heavy overcoat and boots that made it difficult to haul him aboard the lifeboat.

In the confusion, they spotted the U-Boat on the surface and Patrick Kearney estimated that it was only 30 yards away with men on the conning tower watching in silence. Despite pleas for help, none was given.

The U90 did witness the explosion and reported that the impact was so strong that the forward hatch cover was blown off and took in water. It came to the surface and passed the wreck position. The Germans saw the CARLINGFORD approaching and making a closer inspection. Jess overestimated the DUNDALK tonnage at 6000tons, it was actually 794 tons, and assumed the steamer was carrying munitions. This was probably his attempt to inflate his tonnage figures since the U-Boat commanders were in competition with each other.

Capt Hugh O'Neill

A steamer, the SS CARLINGFORD, passed very close to them during the aftermath and Kearney and others again shouted for help. The steamer eased up after 150 yards and looked for survivors but unfortunately did not stop to throw a line and haul the survivors on board. The seven men in this lifeboat faced the arduous task of just keeping her afloat and themselves alive. They put up a flag of distress, an old blanket attached to an oar and the ill gunner, Ferguson, helped them navigate by using a compass. They rowed for hours in the direction of Anglesey and it was not until the following day at 4.30 pm that they were spotted by a seaplane, which alerted the Admiralty. The trawler STORMCOCK, under the command of Captain Norton, appeared and took the men to Holyhead. These men were lucky to be alive after 17 hours on the open sea; the trawler crew and officials at Holyhead provided them with every comfort. Lieutenant Green allowed them to sleep on the Mail Boat.

S.S. DUNDALK CREW LIST 1918

NO.	NAME	AGE	RANK	NOTES
1	Hugh O'Neill	53 yrs.	Master	Lost
2	John Higgins	34 yrs.	2nd Mate	Saved
3	Patrick Melia	48 yrs.	AB	Lost
4	Daniel Stowell	29 yrs.	QM (First Ship)	Lost
5	William McKeown	56 yrs.	AB	Lost
6	Patrick McCourt	24 yrs.	AB	Saved
7	Patrick Byrne	29 yrs.	AB	Saved
8	Francis Kieran	19 yrs.	AB	Lost
9	Pat Moonan	38 yrs.	AB	Saved
10	Vincent Morgan	20 yrs.	Greaser	Lost
11	Joseph Fox	30 yrs.	Cattleman	Lost

12	Peter Sloane	19 yrs.	OS (First Ship)	Lost
13	Edward Johnston	40 yrs.	Chief Engineer	Lost
14	John Mulqueen	44 yrs.	2nd Engineer	Saved
15	Thomas Fitzgerald	38 yrs.	Winchman	Saved
16	John Muckian	45 yrs.	Fireman	Lost
17	Edward Bennett	40 yrs.	Fireman	Lost
18	James Hernon	38 yrs.	Fireman	Lost
19	Thomas Tuite	20 yrs.	Donkeyman	Lost
20	Hugh O' Neill	41 yrs.	Fireman	Saved
21	Patrick Hughes	39 yrs.	Fireman	Lost
22	John Stacks	31 yrs.	Fireman (First Ship)	Lost
23	Joseph Halpenny	38 yrs.	Fireman	Lost
24	Peter Matthews	43 yrs.	Steward	Lost
25	Margaret Creegan	33 yrs.	Stewardess	Lost
26	Patrick Kearney	35 yrs.	Cattleman	Saved
27	Francis Deery	43 yrs.	Cattleman	Saved
28	James Tuite	45 yrs.	Cattleman	Saved
29	Timothy Connor		RNR Gunner	Saved
30	Angus Ferguson	45 yrs.	RNR Gunner	Saved
31	Harold Grey	18 yrs.	RNVR 2nd Gunner (First Ship)	Lost
32	Samuel John Cocks	48 yrs.	Manager	Lost

(I have taken this list from Sarah Toale's return for the Board of Trade.)

FOR GOD'S SAKE DON'T LEAVE US!

There were five other survivors in another lifeboat, which had drifted away from the other one in the confusion, darkness and trauma of the sinking. They too had noticed the U-Boat on the surface with two to three men on the conning tower, maybe 30 yards away, where it lurked in silence for five minutes before disappearing into the darkness. Patrick Moonan said that at the time they saw the U-Boat on the surface the SS CARLINGFORD came upon the scene and nearly ran them over. He hailed this vessel for help but the ship was steered hard to starboard after going some distance and failed to return.

The CARLINGFORD could have alleviated the suffering of the survivors but steered clear probably because they feared another torpedo strike. It was not unknown for the U-Boats to attack the rescue vessels in the later stages of the war. The U-Boat commander, Heinrich Jess, who claimed this kill offered no help and survived the war. He lived until 1962. There was no repeat of Otto Hersing's chivalry and humane decision of 1915 to commandeer another ship for rescue purposes.

The men in this lifeboat endured the same degree of hardship as their colleagues. Moonan said that they ran before the wind until daylight in a short choppy sea and then they made a sail out of a blanket and a jury mast out of an oar. They were starving, exhausted, cold, constantly bailing and rowing towards the Welsh coast. After 16 hours in the lifeboat, they were picked up about 25 miles from Liverpool by the SS DOUGLAS, with Captain Kelly in charge, and landed at the Isle of Man. The five men in this lifeboat were Thomas Fitzgerald, Hugh O'Neill, John Mulqueen, Patrick McCourt and Patrick Moonan. Mulqueen had survived because he went on deck to oil a dynamo. Three others had escaped from the forecastle that was some distance from the explosion. American and British destroyers were still looking for the U-Boat which sunk the LEINSTER and now the DUNDALK. There was a massive search along the mail route and the Irish Sea was broken down into sectors for search purposes. Airships and Auxiliary Patrol Vessels with hydrophones were also used but the U90 escaped the depth charges. The UB123 was not so fortunate and may have ran into a minefield further north with the loss of all hands.

CONCLUSION

When I found the crew list for the SS DUNDALK for the day of the disaster, I turned over the page and found an interesting note about the other crewmembers who 'fortunately' missed the attack. At this time, Ireland, especially Dublin and Dundalk, was being ravaged by an influenza epidemic often accompanied by septic pneumonia. Thousands of people had died and hundreds had been buried in Glasnevin Cemetery that October already. A direct result of the flu epidemic and the victims of the LEINSTER attack. There were over 1,100 cases of influenza in Dundalk town and medical staff were at full stretch. In many cases entire households had been laid up and businesses had to close. Local schools and theatres were also shut in an effort to stop the spread. To give you some idea of the gravity of the situation, the Urban District Council of Newry issued a public notice about the influenza epidemic. This was designed to stop the spread of infection and stated thus 'The Urban District Council acting as the Public Health Authority have been advised to PREVENT THE HOLDING OF 'WAKES' in the case of persons who have died from Influenza or from any complication arising out of same and to insist on the early burial of such persons'. There were also warnings about repeated dosing using spirituous liquors and large gatherings in public places. Churches were disinfected and the picture palaces closed.

On the 8th October, eleven men were taken from the SS DUNDALK at Dundalk suffering from influenza.

They were all Dundalk men and listed as:

James Higgins (33) Mate, Robert Moyston (20) Able Seaman, Thomas Halpenny (34) Trimmer, Patrick Roddy (38) Winchman, John Carrol (31) Quarter Master, Patrick Muckian (35) Greaser, James McGuinness (30) Fireman, Bernard McCabe (43) Cattleman, John Hall (17) Ordinary Seaman and W. Tuite (48) Donkeyman.

Substitutes had to be found for these men and also for Patrick Hanratty, a Fireman from Warrenpoint who was taken ashore with a similar complaint at Liverpool on the 9th October 1918, a few days before the no warning attack. His coffin was on the SS DUNDALK when she was torpedoed. Although some of these men later died from the influenza outbreak, it was a case of the lesser of two evils and certainly the luck of the draw.

The sinking of the SS DUNDALK had unleashed a backwash of grief, anger, sympathy, faith and hope in the town.

On Tuesday the 22nd October 1918, a fund was set up by the company and Cardinal Logue in Dundalk Town Hall to aid the dependents of the victims of the sinking, especially the children. A resolution of sympathy for the families was expressed and the fund was kick-started by the company with a £500 donation followed by generous donations from all present of £25 or £50 by local traders and dealers. £2,000 was raised on the night and the appeal was extended to the general public to provide relief for the children of the victims who were left fatherless. This fund eventually raised £6,000 for the dependants.

Hugh O'Neill's body was never found and there was no satisfactory closure for the family. Annie was left to cope with her grief with the support of her family and townsfolk, like Sarah Toale, who did a lot for the bereaved. She survived financially and maintained the link with Killowen. The two sons, Sonny and Vin, did not venture to sea.

Sara Toale, daughter of an R.I.C. Sergeant, worked for the Steam Packet Company in Dundalk as Secretary and became the Honorary Secretary of the Dundalk Fund. Her work on behalf of the bereaved was recognised by the relatives of those who perished on the SS DUNDALK and the framed ADDRESS from them is in the Dundalk Museum as a mark of their respect and gratitude. This was presented to her exactly a year after the sinking. She ensured that the interests of the bereaved were protected and that they received their entitlement from the Workman's Compensation Act, War Pensions Fund and the Dundalk Disaster Fund. Annie O'Neill signed this address to a remarkable lady. Winchman Patrick Roddy, who was 20 years on the DUNDALK, had died from influenza and was buried on the same day that the DUNDALK was torpedoed. He left a widow and large family and the Dundalk Fund Committee decided to make them an allowance also.

The five direct descendants of Hugh and Annie O'Neill are to be found today in Dundalk, Dublin and County Laois. They include Des Casey and Kevin O'Neill in Dundalk, Maureen Kelly and Anne Howard in Dublin and Patricia Shiels in County Laois. Another descendant, Hugh O'Neill Casey sadly passed away in May 2009.

The Dundalk Sub Aqua Group dived to the shipwreck in 2010 and they reported that the ship is lying about 60 metres deep in two sections with the bow and stern separate indicating that the torpedo split the ship in two. There is a long deck section visible and two boilers. The club made sure the victims were not forgotten on the 92nd Anniversary and laid a commemorative plaque at the site of the wreck. Some artefacts were taken to Dundalk Museum for display purposes and can be viewed there.

SS DUNDALK Portholes on display in County Museum Dundalk

In the cross-channel trade gap left by the loss of the SS DUNDALK, the Company bought the SS KITTIWAKE as a replacement in early 1919. She was fitted out to carry sheep and pigs between Newry and Liverpool. By September 1919 at their Annual Meeting, the Company was able to report a financial profit, but an emotional profit was harder to come by. Tributes were paid to the crew of the SS DUNDALK and there was special mention of Captain Hugh O'Neill from Killowen. He was remembered as an efficient seaman and honourable man who had shown great valour and seamanship when chased by a submarine in 1917.

There is also a plaque and stained-glass window in Dundalk Cathedral, which honours the dead. There are 19 names on the plaque with one name, Mr. Harold Grey from Swansea, missing. These people were cruelly taken too soon near the end of a long war where both sides preyed on the merchant ships. The people of Dundalk have ensured that the victims of the sinking are not forgotten and as we approach 2018 these memories will become more poignant. There are more stories to tell.

In London on the Tower Hill Merchant Navy Memorial the names include Harold Grey, but Mr Samuel John Cocks, the manager is omitted, as he was not a Merchant Seaman.

SS DUNDALK

SOURCES OF INFORMATION

I am grateful for the help given to me by the following people, friends, organisations and written sources.

1 Dundalk Democrat 23rd March 1918; 19th October 1918

2 Dundalk Examiner & Louth Advertiser 26th October 1918

3 Irish News 22nd October 1918

4 Irish Independent 22nd October 1918 (includes photos on page 5)

5 Tempest's Annual 1918-24; Tempest's Annual 1968 (IR94132TI) National Library Dublin

6 'Faces from the Past' Merchant Seamen from Dundalk in the Early 20th Century. David Snook, County Museum Dundalk

7 1901 and 1911 Census of Ireland

8 National Archives Kew. ADM 137/2964; BT110/291

9 Anita Barrett County Museum Dundalk (Photographs of SS DUNDALK Courtesy of Old Dundalk Society)

10 Dundalk Irish Historic Towns Atlas No. 16 by Harold O'Sullivan, Royal Irish Academy, 19 Dawson St, Dublin. (2006)

11 Anne Howard, Dublin for her detailed history of Hugh O'Neill and his family

12 Mary O'Neill and Eileen Ryan, Killowen for providing O'Neill family details and photographs

13 Charlie McCarthy, Dundalk & Sean Rickard, Limerick

14 Dr Royan Norton, Belfast

15 Alan Napier, London & Dr Noëlle McCavana

16 'Dear Daughter = The Messenger Letters. Voyages of a Sailing Ship Captain 1890 – 1898'. Edited by Graham Hindle. Published by John Gray Books, Blackburn

17 Des Casey and Kevin O'Neill in Dundalk

18 'Death in the Irish Sea, The Sinking of the R.M.S. LEINSTER'. Roy Stokes. The Collins Press, Cork. 1998

19 PRONI, Belfast. Shipping Records for S.S. ULIDIA & S.S. BESSBROOK

20 Dundalk & Newry Steam Packet Company Steamers (D.& N.S.) (Courtesy of Dundalk Library)

21 Staff in Dundalk Library, especially the Irish Heritage Section

22 'Down the Quay' A History of Dundalk Harbour
A Book produced by a local team in 1988 -
available for reference in Dundalk Library
The author would like to point out that the DUNDALK ~ ANNIE CROSSFIELD collision mentioned in this book took place in 1906 and not 1914. Captain Berrill was in charge of the DUNDALK at this time and he did rescue the crew of the schooner. There was no loss of life.

23 'Hostile Sea' U-Boat Offensive around the Isle of Man WW1
Adrian Corkill Mannin Printing, Isle of Man 2013

Erected in Memory of those Mariners from Mourne who have lost their lives in pursuit of their calling

Kilkeel Memorial

Erected at the Nautilus Centre, Kilkeel Harbour

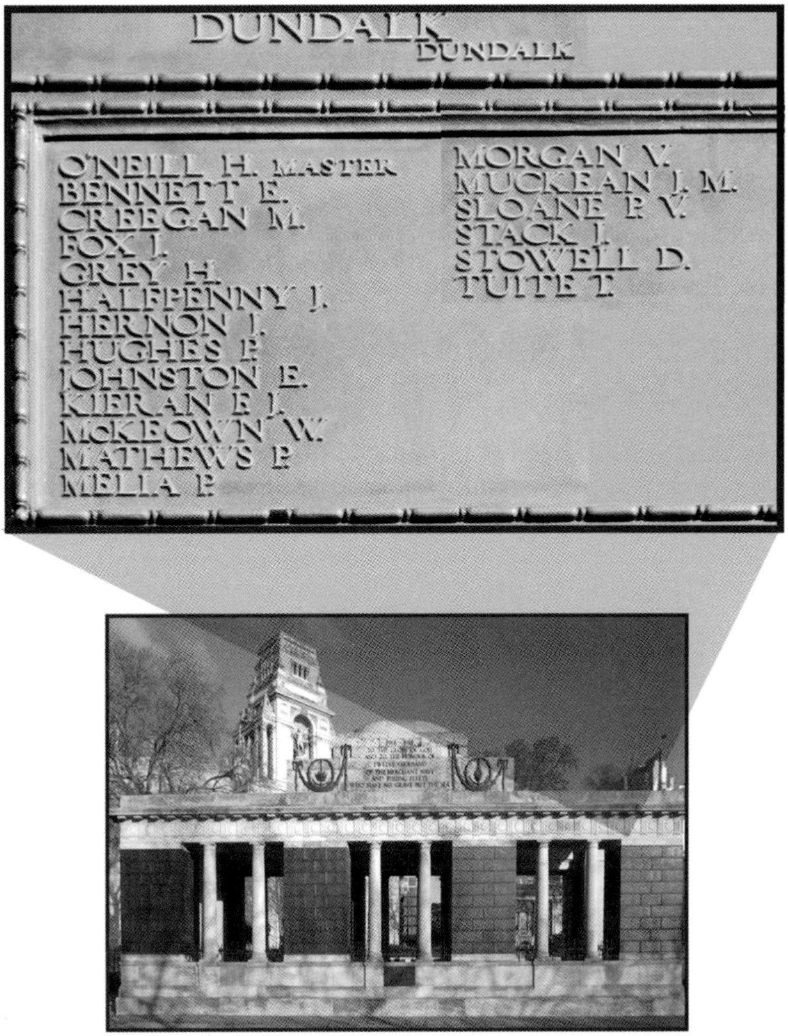

Merchant Navy Memorial, Tower Hill, London

1914 –1918
TO THE GLORY OF GOD
AND TO THE HONOUR
OF TWELVE THOUSAND
OF THE MERCHANT NAVY
AND FISHING FLEETS
WHO HAVE NO GRAVE BUT THE SEA

SOME OF THE D. & N. S. STEAMERS

SS BESSBROOK

SS IVEAGH

SS DUNDALK

Captain Hugh O'Neill started on the SS BESSBROOK IN 1911.

He was killed on the SS DUNDALK in October 1918.

LUCK OF THE DRAW

THE ALPHA

The ALPHA was the first schooner built in Kilkeel Harbour by William Paynter in 1879 and registered in Newry with the official number 69773. Paynter was a famous ship and boat builder from St. Ives in Cornwall. At 38 years of age and seeing a potential market across the Irish Sea for luggers, he decided to set up his boat building business at Kilkeel Harbour to supply local and Manx fishermen in 1875. The ALPHA was owned by Paynter initially (1879—1883) and then passed through the hands of a succession of Kilkeel owners, namely Samuel Shannon (1884—1891); Robert Green (1891—1893); Mrs. S. Shannon (Managing Owner from 1893—1916) and William J. Chambers of Greencastle Street, Kilkeel (1916—1933).

James Maginnis (*Courtesy of Frank Maginnis*)

In 1917 and 1918, James Maginnis (Jimsey) of Harbour Road, Kilkeel was the Master. He later became part owner of the vessel. There were only three crewmembers on board, Jimsey, plus my grand-father, Charlie Maginnis as Mate and Thomas Gray as an AB/Cook. Occasionally the roles of Mate and Able Seaman (AB) were reversed probably in the interests of fairness, since both men were experienced sailors and played many parts on board this schooner.

Charlie was his younger brother and Thomas was a neighbour. With a ship registered at 61 gross tons and 49 nekt, Jimsey was always on the lookout for cargoes. Voyages depended on the weather, especially wind power and direction, and although the ALPHA was rated a flying machine when conditions were favourable, some trips were lengthy and perilous. In 1917, it could take the ALPHA 20 days to travel from Kilkeel to Birkenhead, 4 days to Maryport or 2 days to Liverpool. She completed 18 voyages to the Mersey, Belfast, Glasgow, Rostrevor and the Cumbrian Coast. In total, she was 75 days at sea. The longer voyages were related to reports of submarine activity in the Irish Sea and stormy weather conditions.

Model of the ALPHA (Courtesy of Frank Maginnis)

There was a similar picture in 1918, with 15 voyages, some lengthy such as Kilkeel to Birkenhead from the 12th January 1918 until 31st January 1918 and some short, like the Kilkeel to Liverpool run on the 23rd April 1918 until the 24th April 1918. Cargoes were composed of coal from Workington, Maryport and Glasgow, potatoes from Kilkeel, scrap iron from Belfast and sand from Campbeltown. Jimsey also managed the difficult route to Millbay with cargoes for the old limekiln.

In all these trips, which criss-crossed the Irish Sea under sail power, Jimsey was one of the lucky ones because he never encountered or even saw a submarine at the height of the unrestricted war!

Philip Torley, Fireman	35	Killowen
William Smartt, Able Seaman	21	Arklow
(Joined 2nd March in Dundalk from SS OPHIR)		
Joined after the incident		
Joseph Garland, Gunner	42	Bristol
(Joined 14th May 1918 from SS ALLENDALE)		
Thomas Robinson, Gunner	18	Northampton
(Joined 14th May from SS DUKE OF CUMBERLAND)		
Bernard McGivern, Ordinary Seaman	18	Newry
(Joined 15th May in Dublin from SS IVEAGH)		
Edward Delaney, Fireman	45	Dublin
(Joined 15th May in Dublin from SAINT PAUL)		
Hugh McVeigh, Able Seaman	21	Annalong
(Joined 15th May in Dublin from AGNES GLOVER)		

Fishers seemed to pay better than some of their competitors with the Master receiving £5 17s 6d per week, the Mate £4 2s 6d per week, Lamp Trimmer £3 19s 6d, AB (Able Seaman) £3 17s 6d, OS (Ordinary Seaman) £2 17s 6d, Chief Engineer £4 17s 6d, 2nd Engineer £3 19s 6d and Fireman £3 17s 6d.

Fishers were lucky during First World War as they operated a number of colliers out of Newry and never lost one to submarine attack. Ships such as the early tree names and local place names such as PORTADOWN and ABBOT plied their trade down Carlingford Lough past the Mournes over the Bar and out into the Irish Sea. They successfully delivered cargoes of coal and, on a less frequent basis, barrels of herring, potatoes, seaweed and stone from Irish ports.

They did have casualties during the war years due to bad weather. The ROSTREVOR foundered at sea on a voyage from Newry to Manchester with a load of granite setts on the 12th April 1917. The UPAS sunk near the South Rock Lightship off the Ards coast on the 17th March 1915. She had been on course for Warrenpoint from Ayr with a load of coal. Gale force winds and driving snow off Portavogie caused the cargo to shift and the UPAS listed badly and sank. There were only two survivors picked up by the Donaghadee lifeboat.

BRAVE MEN – CAPTAIN JAMES KERR & CAPTAIN WILLIAM M^cKIBBIN

Captain James Kerr from Bridge Street, Kilkeel had an unusual encounter with a U-Boat in 1917 in the middle of the English Channel. He went to sea at an early age of 15 years and quickly distinguished himself as a schooner captain by the time he was 21. He was described as a brisk, intelligent mariner with a blue peaked cap, bell-bottomed trousers and a trim white beard. He was the head of a large family and served for nearly 60 years on a variety of schooners such as JOHN CARTMEL, THOMAS, EDITH, AID, OSPREY and the LIZZIE ELLEN. He never owned a schooner but preferred to work for owners in England, Wales, Dundalk and Kilkeel.

In 1916, Captain Kerr was working for Evans and Williams of Cardiff and he was Master of the schooner called YACHT, registered in Bideford at 71 net tons. On the 12th November 1916, he set off from Waterford on what was to become a very eventful voyage. There were four men on board; Captain James Kerr as Master, James Lowe, also from Kilkeel, as Mate, Michael Kent from Arthurstown, County Wexford as Able Seaman (AB) and Evan Lloyd Williams from Holyhead. The cargo was composed of 100 tons of steel horings and 25 tons of scrap destined for Glasgow. This cargo sounds innocuous enough, but for Captain Kerr and his crew it turned out to be a nightmare; and illustrates that there were lethal hazards in addition to the U-Boats.

From the outset of the voyage north from Waterford, the schooner ran into rough weather and had to seek shelter in Ardglass Harbour for a number of days. When the weather moderated sufficiently, James Kerr proceeded north, but again he was beaten by the stress of inclement weather and forced to seek sanctuary in Belfast Lough. By 3.00 am, on November 23rd 1916, the ship was anchored off Whiteabbey, about two miles out. The starboard anchor had been lowered with about 20 fathoms of cable and the anchor lights were burning brightly. When James Kerr came on watch duty, he noticed a peculiar smell like wood burning in addition to the usual rusty stale smell associated with this cargo. He lifted the small boat off the main hatch with the assistance of the AB. The hold was a mass of fire and they quickly replaced the hatch and stretched tarpaulins over it in an effort to cut off the air supply.

All hands were called on deck and the small boat was launched. A line was slacked away from the schooner and the crew held on until 4.30 am when they abandoned the ship and rowed to Whiteabbey Pier. At 7.30 am James Kerr went back on board the burning ship and, with the help of the Captain of the MENAI, cut away the mainsail from the spars and placed it on his vessel. This Captain had already removed a staysail from the YACHT.

In the meantime, Mr Legg's steamer WOODBURN, laden with coal from Maryport, had reached his pier. Captain M^c^Gookin of the WOODBURN was given permission to attempt a rescue of the YACHT. They tried to cut the anchor chain, but this was aborted because the forepart of the schooner was a raging furnace. They then decided to attach a steel hawser to the stricken vessel and tow her, plus the anchor, to Whiteabbey beach. The burning schooner was beached between the pier and the coastguard station by 10.00 am. Half an hour later, the foremast fell on the deck taking the main mast with it.

Men from the wharf tried to bore holes in the schooner to flood the fire, but their efforts were in vain, and by the morning of the 24th November 1916 there was nothing left but the keel and a few smouldering timbers. The small boat, a mainsail and staysail, two compasses, a foghorn and a medicine chest were the only items salvaged by Captain Kerr.

A lot of sailors and local people helped the crew during this incident, which was probably caused by friction creating heat in the steel horings during the lengthy storm-tossed voyage north in the Irish Sea. Whiteabbey folk like Mrs Stevenson and Mrs McClelland of Coastguard Row looked after the crew until their departure. Sergeant Donaghy, R.I.C., also attended the needs of the crew before they left for the Sailor's Home in Belfast. Captain Kerr had to stay in Whiteabbey to make his report to the Receiver of Wrecks. This unusual shipwreck happened just after the BRITTANIC, launched from Queen's Island in 1914, was torpedoed in the Mediterranean Sea. Soon it would be Captain Kerr's turn to meet a U-Boat.

OTTO STEINBRINCK AGAIN!

In January 1917, Captain James Kerr became the Master of the schooner LIZZIE ELLEN, which had been registered in Cardigan. On the 27th June 1917, he left St. Helier on Jersey with a cargo of scrap iron destined for Newport, South Wales. Obviously, he was not put off by the accident on the YACHT! The LIZZIE ELLEN was again owned by Evans & Williams, 36, Mount Stewart Square, Cardiff and it had been chartered by Hurst Brothers, St. Helier. The schooner steered a north-west course across the channel against a light north-west wind of 4 knots. By 2.25 pm on the 28th June, the weather was fine, the sea smooth and visibility 7 miles. Otto Steinbrinck then announced his presence in true dramatic style. He had just moved north from the Mediterranean theatre of war after creating a cluster of sinkings around Cap Ferrat. His attack on the LIZZIE ELLEN was a virtual copy of the one on James Ferguson's EARNEST.

Steinbrinck's UC65, fired three shells at the schooner and one hit the top fore-mast. James Kerr and his crew had to abandon ship after destroying the confidential papers, such as the Sailing Instructions.

The Master was then forced to row the German boarding party over to the LIZZIE ELLEN in his lifeboat. Steinbrinck was obviously a trophy collector because the steering-wheel of the schooner was cut off and the vessel pillaged. The Germans were looking for stores of food and took sugar, potatoes and other food stuffs, as well as the barometer and compass. Was James Ferguson's gift, the binoculars, stolen property from another ship?

Crew List of the LIZZIE ELLEN 1917

[All crew joined in Liverpool 12/1/17]

	Names		Age	Birthplace
1	Captain James Kerr	Master	57 yrs *	Kilkeel
2	Mat Timmins	Mate	46 yrs	Waterford
3	William Butler	AB	22 yrs?	Jamaica
4	James Higgins	OS/Cook	17yrs	Kilkeel

*James Kerr was recorded as 60 years old in the 1911 census. In the 1917 crew lists he gave his age as 57 or 58!

The German boarding party took photographs of the steering-wheel and the schooner before the bombs were planted. James Kerr was in conversation with the Chief Officer who spoke good English. Back on the submarine, he noted a German ensign hoisted near the periscope and two guns, one fore part and one after part of the conning tower. He also saw a wireless mast and described the paint used as slate between the bow and the fore part of the conning tower. Aft the U-Boat was painted black. The fore part had been newly painted and the after part had older paint. He saw 12 to 14 young crew on deck with no distinct uniform. Steinbrinck seemed to be the only one in uniform. More photographs were taken of the crew and the steering-wheel. A story from the descendants of James Kerr from Warrenpoint relates that the Germans wanted to keep Captain Kerr's loyal Jamaican seaman, but Kerr refused to hand him over to Steinbrinck. They were then cast adrift in their small boat with 2 loaves of bread and a kettle of water. By now it was 4.00 pm in the afternoon and the LIZZIE ELLEN was sunk. The U-Boat headed east by southeast, probably returning to their base in Flanders. The schooner was sunk 46 miles south of Start Point (Devon). James Kerr gave the position as 30 miles northwest of the Roches Douvres lighthouse.

The crew of the LIZZIE ELLEN had a fraught night in the lifeboat and were rescued by a Hospital ship at 9.00 am the next morning and landed at Plymouth. James Higgins, the youngest crewmember, was James Kerr's grandson. Shortly after this incident he died in South Wales from peritonitis and was buried in Cardiff.

Captain Kerr was awarded two medals for bravery during his First World War voyages. The Mercantile Ribbon on 13th March 1920 and Mercantile Medal on 5th April 1921. They were given to those who served at sea for no less than 6 months between 4th August 1914 and 11th November 1918 and on at least one voyage through a danger zone. All recipients of the Mercantile Marine Medal were automatically entitled to the British Ribbon and Medal, which were awarded on the same date.

Captain James Kerr continued to sail the seas closer to home and was the Master of the LIZZIE (owned by Robert Skillen of Annalong), SARAH EVANS and the NORTHERN LIGHT. These vessels were involved mostly in the coal trade and discharged their cargo at Kilkeel and Millbay. Captain Kerr died in 1926 as the patriarch of a large family. In the 1970s, Hugh and Martha Kerr still lived in Bridge Street and they maintained a folk music tradition often championed by the family. They had a well-used piano in the house and Hugh was a proficient violinist. I remember his shoe repair shop and his keen interest in greyhounds from the 1960's. The family dispersed to Warrenpoint in the 1970's and one of their descendants, Margaret Harty, helped me with family details.

CAPTAIN WILLIAM M^c^KIBBIN

Captain William McKibbin, was from Annalong and a well-known schooner man. He went to sea when he was 13 years old and the deck became his classroom for learning navigational skills. He served his time on schooners and steamboats. He had spells on the BROOKSIDE and RIVERSIDE steamers and then moved on to captain the OLD HUNTER, MARY GRACE, HOWARD and TEXA. The one schooner he was primarily associated with was the NELLIE BYWATER from 1921 to 1945. This schooner was taken over by the Admiralty in 1940 to assist in the war effort with William McKibbin in charge. It was much altered in appearance with the bowsprit and mainmast removed and the fiddle bow cut off. The sailing vessel operated around Belfast Lough and acted as a tender taking cargo and equipment to the larger transports. As the war progressed, this converted ship became a mobile degaussing workshop and a fuel ship for the Navy's Light Coastal Forces. After restoration, Captain McKibbin's famous ship was sold to Captain Richard English who was a renowned schooner man. Under his stewardship the old sailing vessel featured in two films, 'The Elusive Pimpernel' with David Niven and 'Circle of Danger' with Ray Milland.

William McKibbin
(Courtesy of
Roy McKibbin)

During the First World War, Captain McKibbin was a younger man in his thirties and in 1918 he was Master and Owner of the HOWARD, a small ketch of 63 tons. On the 24th February 1918, Captain McKibbin came across a Norwegian steamer, which had been torpedoed by the U105 (Kapitänleutnant Friedrick Strackerjan). The SARPFOS steamer was on a northward voyage from Swansea to Stornoway and Odda, under the charge of the Master, Hans Johannssan. The torpedo attack took place north of the Skerries, near Anglesey and 14 miles SW by S of the Calf of Man. This was a no warning strike and the lookout only saw the track of the silver fish before it exploded on the port side. The recommendation to zigzag had not been followed by this neutral ship in a war zone. The torpedo exploded at the bulkhead between the engine room and the stokehold about two feet below the water line. The engine room and boiler room were wrecked and the port lifeboat was blown to pieces. There were two casualties in this attack, a Donkeyman in the engine room and a Fireman in the stokehold. The remainder of the crew of 20 and one passenger abandoned ship in the starboard lifeboat and were rescued by the HOWARD with William McKibbin and William John McKee on board about an hour later. Captain McKibbin offered to take them to Liverpool and the Norwegian Captain took up this offer as the wind and sea were rising. This was a risky venture because the U105 deck gun could easily have sunk the HOWARD.

The Royal Norwegian Navy recognised his bravery and seamanship and presented him with a silver cup, which the captain proudly displayed in Bywater House, Annalong. The inscription when translated read:

'the Thanks of the Norwegian Board of Trade to Captain William McKibbin, Master of the HOWARD in recognition of his bravery and seamanlike qualities in rescuing the crew of the Norwegian ship SARPFOS of Christiania (Oslo) which had been sunk by a German submarine off the Skerries near Anglesey.'

This was a courageous Mourne Man who was awarded medals in both World Wars. He retired from his maritime adventures after the Second World War at the age of 73. A well respected resident of Annalong, he was fond of his garden and a regular church attendee in his retirement years. A modest sincere gentleman, he never boasted of his wartime achievements. He died on the 28th August 1952 and his funeral to Kilhorne Church in Annalong was one of the biggest in Mourne. It seemed appropriate that the film 'Elusive Pimpernel' had been playing in the Vogue Cinema, Kilkeel just after his funeral.

Bywater House, Annalong 2012

SS RIBBLETON MYSTERY

William John McKee who helped in the rescue of the Norwegian merchantmen in 1918 met an untimely death in January 1919 after the war. There is still a lot of mystery attached to his disappearance. I spoke to Gertie and Archie Orr about the loss of the SS RIBBLETON and fortunately they were keen family historians who had research material on the McKee family of Harbour Road, Kilkeel. William John McKee had been on board the RIBBLETON when the ship disappeared. Samuel McKnight & Co. had built this steamer of 299 gross tons in Ayr in 1887. She was about 145 feet long by 22.5 feet wide, clincher built and schooner rigged. Formerly, her name was YARE and then NORFOLK. In 1919, she was owned by Joseph Gale of 7, Woodplumpton Road, Ashton-on-Ribble, County Lancaster. Her name was finally changed to RIBBLETON on the 9th August 1915.

After leaving Kilkeel Harbour with a cargo of potatoes on 8th January 1919, the steamer disappeared and the mystery was what happened to her and the crew who were all deemed lost at sea. When William John McKee boarded this steamer, he was filling in for a friend whose wife had some kind of premonition about the voyage ahead. William John's wife, Susan, noticed that he had left his favourite purple silk handkerchief behind. His daughter Peg was sent down to the harbour with the handkerchief but when she got there the steamer had already left, creating a maritime mystery with no satisfactory closure for the families of the crewmembers.

William John McKee and his wife Susan
(*Courtesy of Archie Orr*)

The weather was fine when she left Kilkeel but there was a severe storm raging on the 9th January. One body was washed up at Castleton on the Isle of Man and was later identified as crewmember John Barker of Preston. Another Kilkeel man on board was a seaman named, Robert James Cousins, of Harbour Road. His father had been in the R.N.R. (Royal Naval Reserve) and died of illness connected to active service in 1917. Archie Orr told me there

The SS BARCHAN was the last victim to be sunk in the Irish Sea during the First World War. This steamer was owned by J. & A. Gardiner & Company and she had left Ayr on the 21st October 1918 for Dublin with 370 tons of coal on board. She was torpedoed at 7.30 pm, four miles from St. John's Point, and eight of the ten crew were lost when the torpedo exploded on the port side causing the ship to sink immediately. Two survivors were picked up from a waterlogged boat by the U.S.S. LAKE CAPENS and landed at Belfast.

A lot of men died at sea during the so-called 'Great War' but on land the carnage was of a different scale. The war lasted four years and three months or 1,560 days. On average, the daily casualty rate of the British Army was approximately 2,000, of these more than 400 a day were killed in action. One of these was Andrew Mulholland, my great uncle, from Kilkeel who had joined the Royal Irish Fusiliers in 1914; he fought with the regiment around Ypres and St. Eloi in 1915. The regiment had been subjected to shell bombardment, hand to hand fighting, snipers, the threat of gas attack and the lottery of trench warfare. He had arrived in France just before Christmas and after the Second Battle of Ypres he was killed in action on the 14th May 1915. His body was buried on the battlefield and his parents were finally informed of his death on the 29th May 1915. He was one of the first men from Kilkeel to be killed in the First World War and his name is carved on the Menin Gate as a lasting memorial to his sacrifice.

NOT

FORGOTTEN

SOURCES OF INFORMATION

I am grateful for the help given to me by the following people, friends, organisations and written sources.

1 'Schoonerman'
By Captain Richard English, 1981 Penguin
This book contains an excellent section on the NELLIE BYWATER from 1873 – 1945

2 'British Shipping Fleets'
Editors Roy Fenton and John Clarkson
Ships in Focus Publications, 2000. This book contains a section on Joseph Fisher and Sons by Roy Fenton and Sean Patterson

3 Mourne Observer 12th April 1968

4 Mourne Observer 15th December 1967

5 'Sailing Ships of Mourne' – Mourne Observer
(Note: The ELLEN ANN named in this book should have been the LIZZIE ELLEN as per Official Records)

6 German Submarine Warfare 1914-1918, In the Eyes of British Intelligence. By Hans Joachim Koerver

7 Roy McKibbin, Bywater House, Annalong

8 Archie Orr, Kilkeel

9 Frank & John Maginnis, Kilkeel

10 Frank Maginnis, Model of Alpha

11 Dr Royan Norton, Belfast. Sketch of Alpha

12 John Fisher, Warrenpoint

13 Sean Patterson, Newry

14 Howard Forsythe, Kilkeel

15 Margaret Harty & Kilian Higgins, Warrenpoint

16 National Archives, Kew, London ADM137/3994; ADM137/2962; BT99/3286

L

M

NELLIE BYWATER
(Courtesy of Roy McKibbin)

Victoria Locks on the Newry Canal

Ships sailed up the Newry River to the lock gate
into the lock and out into the Newry Canal heading for Newry
(note the canal is higher than the river)

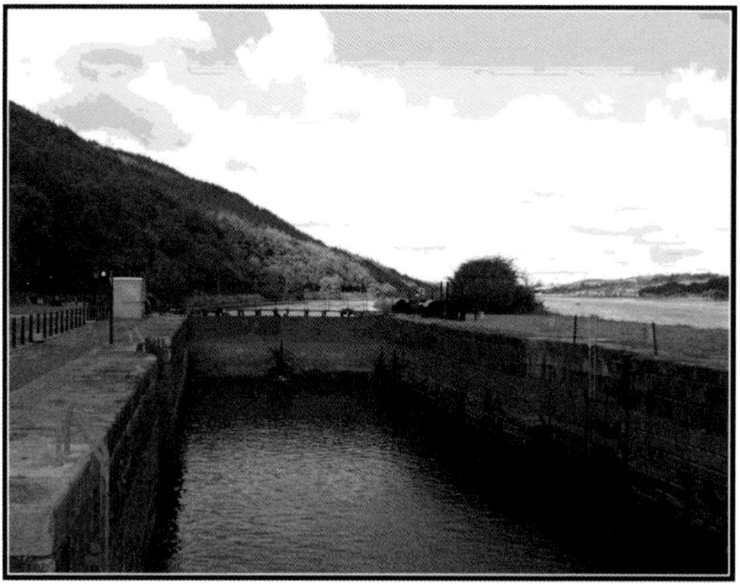